Zambia Shall Be Saved

The Nevers Mumba Story

Written By Kirbey Lockhart

DR. NEVERS MUMBA
TEL: +260-96-994585.

Written by Kirbey Lockhart
Box 1780
Lethbridge, Alberta T1J 4K4
Canada
(403) 320-1565
kirbey@canada.com
www.victorylethbridge.ca

ISBN 0-9688506-0-X

Printed in Canada by
Paramount Printers Ltd.
Lethbridge, Alberta

FOREWORD

It was the first "big" convention at our Bible school in Germany. Pastors were coming from everywhere, it seemed. The director of the German school gave me a list of speakers. There was one name I didn't recognize. "It's Nevers Mumba from Zambia, Africa, who just finished two years at Christ For the Nations Institute in Dallas,"said the director. I didn't personally know him, had never heard him speak, and expressed my concern. "Wait till you hear him," the director added. I did.

When Nevers rose to speak, here was an articulate, anointed young man who ministered with authority through the Word, which gave him an immediate, attentive audience. Impressive to say the least!

Nevers had, after graduation, returned to Zambia and to Florence, a Christian young lady whom he planned to marry. For two long years, she had waited for him. Now, for one more year, it was her turn to go to Dallas to attend CFNI. Upon her return to Zambia, the couple married and began a ministry together.

But it was Reinhard Bonnke who had earlier visited Zambia where he held a huge, powerful crusade with Nevers as his interpreter. Here it was where Mumba first witnessed powerful miracles that stirred his soul. After the crusade, Bonnke recommended

Nevers attend CFNI in Dallas, which is how God led the Mumbas to attend.

In Zambia, Nevers fasted and prayed for a divine strategy. The training of young men began in his home. The Bible school came next, where many young people would be trained in the Bible, with emphasis on integrity, discipline, purpose, a God-given goal, and dominion in the Holy Spirit. The gifts and lasting fruit of the Holy Spirit were taught to assist the God-called trainees to plant churches. Nevers is often speaking on television and in crusades around the world.

Through the years, Nevers has kept close ties with my son, Dennis and me, and we have watched amazed as his ministry has flourished and touched so many in Zambia as well as other parts of the world.

With the vision, the priorities, the focus and purpose Nevers Mumba has, his writings are inspirational and have my recommendation for reading and studying for a man or woman who desires to make an impact in this life; the goal: to win multitudes to Jesus!

Freda Lindsay
CFNI Co-Founder
May 2000

ENDORSEMENTS

Nevers Mumba is a man of multifaceted gifts and talents. God has truly blessed him by anointing him with the Holy Spirit 'to preach the Gospel to the poor' and to make a difference in the Kingdom of God on earth. More than that, He called Nevers to be a 'Joseph in Egypt,' by giving him understanding and prominence in the political affairs of his country. Joseph's visions and dreams turned out to be true and became concrete reality, and I pray that it may happen to Nevers as well. Joseph's life also shows that when God blesses a man, everything falls into place, even the wrath of a man. But that is nothing, for 'If God is for us, who can be against us?'

Reinhard Bonnke, Frankfurt, Germany

There are numerous examples where God's sovereign hand selected someone who seemed to be the least likely to impact history. God, of course, is looking at the individual's heart rather than someone who looks the part. Nevers Mumba is such an individual, coming from a past with little going for him other than an intense passion to know his God and to make Him known. As a result, God selected Nevers to be a spokesman to his generation and to his nation. Only God knows the impact that this fervent young preacher will have on his continent for the glory of God.

Dennis Lindsay, President and CEO, Christ For The Nations

I first met Dr. Nevers Mumba twenty years ago. Already then as a very young man, he demonstrated outstanding leadership. Today, he is a visionary leader, who has not only a great zeal for God, but also wisdom, servanthood and integrity in dealing with his fellow man.

Pastor Peter Youngren, St. Catharines, Ontario, Canada

When I first met Dr. Mumba, there was one distinct characteristic that emanated from his life and that was humility. He is a man who stands on his God-given authority, but yet the same humility that Jesus Christ walked in.

He is a leader of leaders and father to many people. He is able to meet people where they are and minister the love and compassion needed.

Dr. Mumba has a determination within him to see the will of God accomplished in his nation of Zambia.

As Jesus said what the Father told Him to say and did what the Father told Him to do, when you come in contact with Dr. Mumba you will find this is a way of life for him. He will not compromise.

Dr. Mumba's passion will continue to drive him on until he hears from the One he loves so dear, "Well done thou good and faithful servant."

Sue McDermott, personal secretary to Dr. Nevers Mumba

Powerful, dynamic, captivating, exhilarating, challenging, uplifting and relevant describe the preaching that Pastor Nevers Mumba brings to North America. How has this 'African preaching machine' acquired such wisdom and gifting? What is the secret to his success? These questions and more are answered in this testimony of the incredible grace and favour of our Lord Jesus Christ. I highly recommend it.

Dr. Olalekan Oluwole Akinremi, University of Manitoba

Nevers Mumba represents the new face of Christian statesmanship in Africa. He has over the years nurtured his primary evangelistic call and passion into a mission that provides a holistic response to the needs of the people God has sent him to.

My encounters with him reveal a very passionate and deeply reflective Christian gentleman who has been gifted by God with a unique ability to express spiritual thoughts with human clarity. His messages are able to cut across the racial and religious divides of our world through their practical application of God's Word.

Nevers has over the years allowed his experiences in life to mature him into a sensitive and compassionate leader, with a hands-on approach to providing positive responses to our continent's often perplexing challenges.

I am confident that the African continent will be enriched by the deployment of the treasures deposited in the bosom of this gifted servant of the Most High God.

I am certainly honored to call him a brother and a friend.

Pastor Mensa Otabil, Accra, Ghana

AUTHOR'S PREFACE

When we reflect back on our days together at CFNI, Nevers often says that I believed in him before he believed in himself. Perhaps that is true. Perhaps that is why I agreed to write this book; I firmly believe that Pastor Nevers Mumba would make a great Zambian president.

I want to thank Melody Bellinghausen D.O., Ryan Thulien C.A., and Peter and Lindyl Pankonin for their conscientious assistance in editing manuscripts. Thank you also to all those who assisted financially on this project.

Finally, I dedicate this book to the warm, smiling people of Zambia. I pray that what is written on the following pages may inspire you to cross the bridge with Nevers into a better tomorrow. **You shall know the truth, and the truth shall make you free** (John 8:32).

TABLE OF CONTENTS

I have enough preacher in me to be a politician, but
do I have enough politician in me to be a preacher?

Anonymous

1

THE BRIDGE BUILDER

Nevers Mumba likes boxing. Yet it would appear almost ungodly for a pastor to enjoy preaching and punching. Clergymen are "men of the cloth," but they are not all cut from the same cloth. Such is the case with Nevers. He is peculiar. His first name is peculiar (the "r" is silent). There has never been a Zambian minister quite like him, for Pastor Mumba is not afraid to step into the ring and fight. . .

> *I am not afraid to fight for a better and free Zambia. I am not afraid to fight against poverty, oppression and hunger. This is a fight I am ready to fight, even alone. The church song says 'Though none go with me, still I will follow.' I shall follow God's will for my life and for my country. I shall not give up until Zambia is saved.*
>
> - *I don't want their (the government's) money unless every Zambian can share it.*
> - *I don't need any favours unless every Zambian will be favoured.*
> - *I don't need any special privileges unless every Zambian can share them.*
>
> *Like many Zambians, I am not happy in Zambia because of suffering and lack of opportunity. I am not happy with the electoral process. I am not happy with the corruption levels. The only thing I am happy with is the prospect of change. We can make a difference. We can change things.*[1]

> *I have made up my mind that I am going to play my part to sensitise*[2] *my generation to the fact that if we want a better country in the next century, we must start to plan now. I have refused to succumb to the intimidation of Government because I have a real cause for concern. You and I can change the future of this nation. With God on our side, victory is certain.*

[1]Speech by National Citizens' Coalition Chairman, Dr. Nevers Mumba, at Kabwe NCC Rally 26 November 1999.

[2]Zambians use British English. Hence, to North American readers some words in this book will seem misspelled.

> *I say to my countrymen and women, wipe away your tears and let us cross over this bridge to a land of opportunity and personal responsibility. Hold my hand and let us cross to the other side. We can change Zambia and we are changing it.*[3]

How can Nevers honestly be so optimistic about the future of his land-locked, third world, African nation? Surely he knows that one in five Zambians has AIDS.

And just what bridge is Nevers inviting others to cross with him? He must have inside information.

[3]7 September 1998 speech by Dr. Nevers Mumba at the Solwezi Press Club.

ZAMBIA'S PASTOR

I have enough preacher in me to be a politician. . .

2

THE YELLOW TENT

Night after night the colossal yellow tent was crammed with 10,000 expectant Zambians. The air was rank, the atmosphere electric. It seemed anything was possible beneath that miracle canvas. People walked for kilometres to get there and stayed late into the night worshipping God. Although Nevers Mumba had heard of Reinhard Bonnke, the famous German healing evangelist, it was altogether different to be in his crusades, and this is precisely where the 21-year-old Nevers found himself in the fall of 1981.

Bonnke, venerated as *the* Apostle to Africa, and his ministry team, Christ For All Nations (CFAN), were conducting tent crusades throughout Zambia, starting in Kitwe in the Copperbelt[4] north and concluding in Livingstone in the south. Countless people received Christ, and were water-baptized, filled with the Holy Spirit, and healed during those exciting weeks. Canadian missionary Gary Skinner was one of the ministers who coordinated the 1981 CFAN outreach and it was he who asked Nevers, then a youth leader at the local Assembly of God church, to be Reinhard's interpreter, beginning in Kitwe. Nevers took the interpreting assignment seriously, for he not only wanted to please God, he wanted to please Reinhard, too. If Reinhard shook his head, Nevers shook his head. If Reinhard paced, Nevers paced. Nevers endeavoured to emulate Reinhard's every action. This interpreting experience forever changed Nevers' life. As he passionately interpreted Reinhard's profoundly simple and simply profound messages into Bemba, the most predominant language in Zambia after English, the young Zambian saw the effect simple faith had on his people. "When you stepped into that tent," Nevers would describe later, "you stepped into another world where anything was possible. People did not want to leave. The singing was climactic. I had never seen anything like it before."

[4]This Zambian province, which borders the Democratic Republic of Congo, produces enough copper to keep Zambia amidst the largest copper-producing nations in the world.

The crusade in the city of Kabwe stands out most in Nevers' mind. Kenneth Meshoe, then the Associate Evangelist on the CFAN team, and now a pastor of a huge church in South Africa and a member of parliament as well, preached all the meetings in Kabwe while Reinhard was back in Europe. Unusually high numbers of healings and miracles occurred under Meshoe's ministry in Kabwe.

Since Bemba is not as commonly spoken in the southern provinces, Mumba was not needed to interpret for Pastor Bonnke there. Nonetheless, the highly impressionable Nevers travelled with the CFAN team and ministered among them in the Lusaka and Livingstone crusades. Nevers found himself addicted to the power and presence of God.

Reinhard had taken note of Nevers' infectious zeal and encouraged him to go to Bible School for further training. Nevers had already received an acceptance letter from a Theological Institute in the West Indies, but Bonnke had other ideas. He told Nevers, "I know nothing about that college, but I know something about Christ For the Nations Institute (CFNI) in Dallas, Texas. It is a school that will complement your ministry and not take away." Upon returning to CFAN's office in South Africa, Reinhard procured a CFNI application form and promptly mailed it to Nevers. Furthermore, Pastor Bonnke sent $1,000[5] to CFNI to pay for Nevers' first semester, encouraging Dr. Freda Lindsay, the president of the school, to accept this young Zambian evangelist into their fall 1982 enrollment.

But August was ten slow months away. Like the Old Testament prophet Jeremiah, Nevers had "fire in his bones," so he began to preach Pastor Bonnke's messages throughout the Copperbelt. People in secondary schools, hospitals, bus stops, jails and market squares became temporary congregations for this fiery Zambian with altar calls for salvation and healing made at the conclusion of every message. 'If Pastor Bonnke did it this way,' Nevers surmised, 'I should, too.' (Nevers has continued this altar call practise ever since.)

In early 1982, Denson Chipasha, Justin Mumba, Boniface Chileshe (late) and other spirit-filled young Zambians teamed up with Mumba to form the fledgling Evangelistic Board of Zambia (EBOZ). They invited a young Canadian evangelist named Peter Youngren to preach at their first crusade. These EBOZ "associate evangelists" continued to preach boldly while Nevers attended

[5]All quotes are in US $, except when referring to the Zambian currency, the *Kwacha*, then a K is used.

Christ For the Nations Institute in Texas and anxiously awaited his return two years later.

Nevers knew that Reinhard had paid for the first semester so all he needed was the plane ticket to Dallas. Kitwe's Murray and Eva Sanderson, "adopted" parents of Nevers, graciously purchased his ticket. After saying good-bye to friends and family, the young evangelist was off to America where a cornucopia of challenges awaited him.

3

NAVY SUITS

As a child, Nevers had shown promise in primary school and was awarded a coveted scholarship to Hillcrest Secondary School in Livingstone, near the picturesque Victoria Falls. His father, Sunday Peter Sekwila Mumba, had attended teacher's college during World War II so it appeared Sunday and Maritha's eleventh child was following along his father's footsteps. From Hillcrest, Nevers could also enroll in the mine's college and become a mining engineer in the Copperbelt. However, the Bonnke crusade had changed everything. Nevers was now consumed with only one thought: Zambia Shall Be Saved!

Not a few Zambians thought this young man lacked foresight in turning down a college education to pursue ministry training in the USA. Concerned friends and family warned Nevers, "Most African pastors are poor and dress terrible." Undaunted, Nevers declined the mine's scholarship and prepared for Bible School. He arrived in Dallas with two suitcases, $200 in his pocket, and a Bible full of promises.

It was there in late August 1982 that our two lives intersected providentially on the 19 hectare (76 acre) CFNI campus. My fiancée Heidi Kuhnert and I had driven to Dallas from British Columbia, Canada, to attend CFNI. After settling into my room at Gordon Lindsay Hall (GLH), I "bumped" into Nevers, who had just settled into his own room. We instantly and permanently became the best of friends.

School was to begin on Sunday, but a special GLH men's service had been planned for that Friday night. One of my earliest recollections of Nevers is of the two of us strolling from GLH to CFNI's Christian Centre and worshipping together in that hall. On our walk back I noticed that while the rest of the young men wore casual shoes, Nevers wore black dress shoes. They were, as I later learned, his only pair. Earlier that day I had purchased a new pair of runners at the Red Bird Mall so I asked Nevers if he wanted my old Adidas. The blue sneakers fit, and he appeared as comfortable in them as we both seemed to feel about our new friendship.

Routine found itself soon enough in Bible School and I found myself spending most of my free time with Heidi and Nevers. Since I had a car and all three of us were new to the southern United States, we drove to places like scenic east Texas to see Last Days Ministries (founder Keith Green had died in a plane crash earlier that summer). Although Last Days was small, their impact through tracts and music had been enormous. We also spent a weekend at Rhema Bible School in Broken Arrow, Oklahoma, visiting a German friend of Nevers, Ekkehard Hornburg. Other students would travel with us as my 1978 Nova could uncomfortably hold six. I will always remember my car full of dozing passengers on our way back to Dallas, except one, an African. Nevers would be in the back seat passing the time praying quietly in the Spirit. If you did not know him, you would think he was mumbling. Nevers has always been that intense, that serious, that disciplined. It is a key to his success.

It was also almost a key to our demise. The rock band, *The Who,* had a concert in early December 1982 at The Cotton Bowl. CFNI sent dozens of students two-by-two to the event to preach and pass out tracts. The school even provided huge signs for us to carry. Nevers and I were partners and our placard read "Only Jesus Fills Emptiness." Nevers was carrying the sign when we passed a grungy group of bikers. The long-haired leader, in stereotypical black leather, was sitting on his bike with his leg in a cast and his woman at his side. He had a cane in his hand. He yelled to Nevers, "Get out of here you nigger." I thought it wise to listen to the man. Nevers thought otherwise. He walked right toward the leader, sign and all. It was one of those rare moments in life when you realise you might die. Thankfully, Nevers turned around and walked away before anything else was said or done. When we were beyond earshot of the bikers, Nevers informed me, "I am not a nigger. I am an African!" To which I replied, "I know, Nevers, but that guy doesn't want to know." I am glad Nevers realised that the difference in semantics, although significant, was not worth dying over.

A highlight of Nevers' first year at CFNI was a visit by Pastor Bonnke. Reinhard preached powerfully to the students at a Tuesday evening service and then spent the next morning with various African students, including Nevers.

The motto then at CFNI stated "The Holy Spirit Teaches at CFNI," and this zealous young man from Zambia evidently registered for the divinity school of hard knocks. Tuition plus room and board for one semester cost more than the $1,000 Reinhard had generously sent CFNI and the school administration was growing increasingly impatient with Nevers' inability to clear his outstanding school bill.

During this faith-testing period, one of CFNI's weekly special speakers called students forward who needed assistance paying their school bill. Along with a few dozen other students, Nevers darted up to the front. The man prayed for the needy students and then graciously offered each of them $100 toward their school bill. After ushers made a hasty head count for the speaker and came up with 70 (it was closer to 110), the evangelist expeditiously wrote a cheque to CFNI for $7,000 then concluded the service. Unfortunately, in the haste, no one made a list of actual student names and over 100 students, including Nevers, went in to claim their $100. The school administration needed the wisdom of Solomon to solve this delicate dilemma and the simple solution they devised worked impartially. Each of the roughly 100 students would pull a piece of white paper and if it had $1 written on it, that fortunate student would receive $100, but if the slip was blank, that student would receive nothing. Nevers spent extra time in prayer that morning asking God to allow him to be one of the 70 students who would pull the $1 piece of paper. Later that day, Nevers walked apprehensively over to the administration building, drew a blank and received nothing. Disheartened, Nevers went back to his room and acquiesced to the growing inevitability of his imminent return to Africa.

Nevers showed so much promise, yet it appeared that his education at CFNI would be aborted.

Both of us chuckle now when we recall this story, but I guarantee it was not funny then. Nevers showed so much promise, yet it appeared that his education at CFNI would be aborted. His plight was too painful to watch, so I helped Nevers out. I called home and talked to my bank and they agreed to mail me a money order that I then gave to Nevers and he, in turn, to CFNI.

As the name implies, Christ For the Nations Institute accepts students from all over the world. Thus, the school created a prudent work/study program for foreign students like Nevers. Essentially, in exchange for tuition, accommodations and a modest monthly stipend, foreign students worked four hours per day on the CFNI campus. International students attended class daily from 8 AM until noon and then worked from 1 PM until 5 PM. This ingenious program allowed Nevers to finish the remaining four semesters, graduating with an Associate of Arts degree in Theology on 13 May 1984.

The work program left Nevers with little free time, but it did develop character, an invaluable commodity in the life of the high-profile minister he would soon become. (Later when Nevers sent his top associates from EBOZ to study at CFNI, he ensured that they, too, were placed on the work/study program.)

In his 1994 book, *Integrity With Fire,* Pastor Mumba reflects on his afternoon job at the CFN[6] Headquarters Building:

> *They told me to clean toilets. In Africa, not everybody cleans toilets. There are different classes there and we've always believed that cleaning toilets was for the lower class. The lady was so joyous and didn't even blush when she told me, "Nevers, this is what you'll be doing. Move the trash out of the offices and make sure all the toilets are cleaned."*
>
> *As I listened to this, I thought I was in the wrong place. I thought, 'Why is she telling me to clean toilets? Is it because I'm from Africa? I'll show her I'm not what she thinks I am.' But after a day or so the Holy Spirit started to show me something. One thought came to me, 'Nevers, if you don't want to clean the toilet, then you should never use it. If you are too high for the toilet, then don't use it. But if you're high enough to use it, you are also high enough to clean it.'*[7]

While studying in Texas, Nevers began to think of a spouse. 'Who back home would make a good pastor's wife?' He mused. 'A pastor needs a wife. This gives his ministry prestige.'

Nevers began mentioning the need for a wife in his letters to Eva Sanderson. Eva in turn recommended Florence Mwape Mwila. Florence had attended the same church in Kitwe as Nevers had and was even in his youth group. She was from a solid, middle-class Christian family. Nevers concurred with Eva that Florence Mwila would make an excellent pastor's wife and was confident that Florence would welcome his offer. Since Bemba culture does not

[6]Christ For the Nations (CFN) is the ministry the late Gordon Lindsay founded in 1948. The Bible school, CFNI, started by Lindsay in 1967, is the most visible ministry of CFN.

[7]Nevers Mumba, *Integrity With Fire* (Tulsa: Vincom Inc., 1994) 29–30.

condone dating as a precursor to marriage, Nevers saved enough money and even more courage to mail an audio tape to Florence, boldly proposing marriage. She responded back by tape, graciously declining his offer. Florence stated that she was happy for Nevers and his opportunity to study overseas, but was definitely not interested in marrying him. Florence went on to say that she would ask God to give Nevers a wife. In spite of the obvious rejection, Nevers prayed and fasted 14 days for Florence Mwila. When the fast ended, Florence called from Kitwe. The Lord had spoken to her and yes, she would marry him.

Nevers and Florence exchanged a plethora of tapes and letters in 1983 and plans were soon in the making for Florence to join her fiancé at CFNI on a one-year work scholarship. It took months to organise but Florence finally arrived in early January, 1984. Heidi and I were married on 21 May, 1983 and were living in the married housing at CFNI when Florence arrived. We drove the nervous Nevers to the Dallas/Fort Worth airport to pick up his fiancée. You can only imagine how awkward it was when Nevers and Florence wanted to go somewhere in the metroplex and I had to chauffeur them. I desperately tried to become invisible until departure time. It worked much better when we went out as couples. The double-date I recall the most clearly was a trip to the Dallas Zoo. Florence had brought matching Zambian outfits and they wore them that day. The two Africans looked stunning together.

Another favourite recollection of Nevers and Florence during their CFNI period was the gymnasium fiasco. School policy forbade students from walking to or from the gym in shorts. Most students wore sweat pants to the gym and then changed into shorts in the change room. One of the married West African pastors saw Florence walking to the gym in her sweat pants and swiftly scolded Nevers. "A pastor's wife must only wear dresses in public, not these American outfits." Submitting to the reprimand, Nevers confronted Florence the next day at school. The ensuing dialogue was lively to say the least! The gym was set up for a missions display where students had to climb, jump, etc.; hardly a place to wear a dress. Florence explained all this to Nevers and also let him know that his comments were neither warranted or appreciated.

On another memorable occasion Florence asked Nevers, "Would you like me to call you 'Ba Sekwila'?"[8] Nevers stated that he wanted to be called 'Ba Sekwila' only if it came from her heart.

> *"Would you like me to call you 'Ba Sekwila'?"*

She replied that it would not be from her heart and has called him Nevers from that day until now. This was a serious breach of Bemba protocol, but Florence had just begun her crusade of disassembling the man-made rules for pastors' wives in Zambia. (After the Mumbas started Victory Bible Church in Kitwe, Florence asked their congregation to show her in the Bible where the pastor's wife must play the piano.)

Since Nevers graduated that May, he and Florence spent but one semester together at CFNI. Consequently, these types of conflicts typified the early stages of their relationship because Nevers and Florence simply did not know each other that well. They were both Africans studying in the USA, they were both struggling financially and they were both determined to be in love with each other.

Florence graduated with a one-year diploma from CFNI on 21 December 1984 and went back to Zambia to plan their wedding. Nevers and Florence were married in Kitwe on 13 April 1985.

Nevers had preached a few times before attending CFNI, but I was a complete beginner. Since we both planned on doing plenty of speaking after graduation, the two of us considered it mandatory to register for the elective course, *Homiletics: the Science and Art of Biblical Preaching*. The loquacious John Garlock, son of the respected African missionary, H.B. Garlock, was our instructor. Over the decades, Garlock's preaching instructions have significantly influenced countless ministers. Pastor Mumba and I are just two examples: Almost twenty years later, Nevers and I still follow the proven principles of message construction and delivery that Brother Garlock taught us at CFNI. Nevers and I often sat together on the chapel pews, soaking up every nugget of wisdom from this seasoned, eloquent speaker. Later, Nevers and I both had to teach homiletics in Bible school settings, and we both used our Garlock notes as a guide. A year or two after Nevers graduated, John Garlock came to Zambia and quickly became a crowd favourite, making several return visits. Nevers still remembers every message that Brother Garlock ever preached in Zambia. I can still recall one of Garlock's favourite quips, "A sermon, to be immortal, does not have to be eternal."

Our instructor dedicated one whole session to the minister's dress and platform decorum. We were told that certain colors like

[8]Nevers' middle name, *Sekwila*, is his Father's name. Keeping the Father's name in the family is a common Bemba tradition. *Ba* is the equivalent of *Mr.*, hence a show of respect to the man and his Father. It is common for Zambian wives to address their husbands in this way.

dark brown are cold, while other colors exude warmth and sincerity, like navy blue. Consequently, Brother Garlock encouraged all future ministers to have a navy or a black suit and to never, ever, wear a green suit on stage. Nevers departed from class rather quietly that day. He only had two suits and they were both green. Neither of us owned a navy suit and it was only weeks before we would be thrust out into gospel ministry. We immediately set out to remedy our problem. Nevers had $0, I had $200. Could we purchase two dark blue suits in Dallas for $200?

Kuppenheimer's, a men's suit store in Irving, often had a "2-Fer" sale. Once in the store, Nevers, Florence and I headed straightway to the navy section of the size 38's. Florence and I soon discovered something amazing about the shape of Nevers' body. For his height he possesses strong, broad shoulders, but tiny hips. Finding a suit to fit Nevers would be a challenge, but he and Florence finally agreed on a 100% polyester suit that was most importantly, navy blue. Meanwhile I had found a polyester/wool solid navy suit for $120 or "2-Fer" $180. The two of us never felt more ready for ministry than when we left the store with our preacher suits in the bag. Heidi posed the two young preachers, clad in navy, with Garlock-approved white shirts and crimson ties, in front of the Institute Building and took a picture. This incident also initiated the practice of Nevers and I periodically dressing the same.

I recall those events like they happened yesterday and I have never regretted spending that extra money to get Nevers that crucial navy suit. Since then at least five suits have been given to me, three coming from that same store, **... for whatsoever a man soweth, that shall he also reap** (Galatians 6:7). A couple years later Nevers gave away his blue suit to a fellow African pastor.

Another prerequisite to ministry is ordination. Fortunately for Nevers, CFN had their own ordaining body. This would allow Nevers to return home as "Reverend Mumba," giving him credibility in the community. Days before graduation, all students who had successfully applied for ordination through CFN were to participate in the ordination service in the chapel. Nevers had invited me to attend. Freda Lindsay gave battle-proven advice about gospel ministry and then read from 2 Timothy 4:2, **Preach the word; be instant in season, out of season. . . .** Each ordination candidate was called up and individually prayed over, with the laying on of hands. When it came time for Nevers to be prayed over, a middle-age female student from Mexico tactfully interrupted the proceedings and prophesied to Nevers, foretelling how much God was going to use him when he returned home to Zambia.

Upon graduating from CFNI, Nevers and fellow-graduate Al Pino took a Lufthansa jumbo jet to Frankfurt. Before coming to CFNI, Pino had been in the US Army, stationed in West Germany. Using his contacts, Al had organized 30 preaching engagements across western Europe for Nevers to minister in. While ministering at a conference at CFNI's sister school in Wolfenbuttal, Germany, CFN President Freda Lindsay heard Nevers Mumba speak for the first time. In her 1984 self-titled book, *Freda*, she recounts that experience:

> *At the conference I met several other CFNI grads: Dynamic Nevers Mumba challenged the conference guests to reclaim their nation for God. He was on his way home to his own communist country. I envision tremendous results in this man's ministry....*[9]

After Germany, Nevers preached in England and Switzerland, then went on to Israel for a quick visit of the Holy Land before flying home via South Africa. His ministry was well received in Europe with significant miracles occurring in several of the services. This experience gave the budding black preacher both much-needed confidence and a taste for international ministry. Nevers realized that his message was not sequestered to Africa. This trip, followed by dozens of other international trips, has exposed Nevers to diverse cultures, allowing him to develop an egalitarian world view.

While boarding a South African Airways (SAA) 747 in Tel Aviv en route to Johannesburg, Nevers found himself being escorted by the flight attendant up front to first class. Smart enough to know not to say anything, the black African flew in style on an *Apartheid* jet. Both the food and the service are already world-renown in SAA's first class, but Nevers received additional pampering from the flight attendants. 'They think I am somebody important,' Nevers smiled to himself. He reclined his huge seat and enjoyed the long flight down Africa.

Sadly, tragic news awaited Nevers in Jo'burg. His Dad had suddenly passed away at the age of 66. Nevers boarded the next available flight to Lusaka, arriving home only to find that his Dad had

[9]Mrs. Gordon Lindsay, *Freda*, (Dallas CFN Publishing, 1984), 150.

been laid to rest the day before. The heat, coupled with poor mortuary refrigerators at the Chinsali Hospital, forced the family to bury Sunday Mumba on the same day he died, 7 August 1984.

Nevers visited his Father's grave site immediately. There was so much he wish he could say to his dad, for like most sons, Nevers wanted to make his father proud of him. Nevers was certain that his dad would want him to be a patriotic, passionate Zambian minister. When Nevers departed slowly from the cemetery, he committed himself to swiftly cover his nation with the Gospel of Jesus Christ. Zambia would never be the same.

4

THE DAY OF SMALL THINGS

To effectively reach his beloved Zambia, Evangelist Nevers Mumba simply duplicated the already-proven ministry paradigms of CFNI and CFAN. With the CFNI educational system still fresh in his mind, Nevers started Victory Bible College in 1985 with four students, Jeston Katebe, Gamaliel Mwanza, Jefferson Sichangwa and Lazarus Myila. Nevers was the first Zambian to start a Bible school in his nation.

From these four students and his faithful EBOZ associates, Nevers created his own crusade team following the model of Bonnke's CFAN. Displaying the alacrity that would soon become Nevers' trademark, Victory Ministries (their new name, replacing EBOZ), or VM, had their first crusade in early 1985, using the Butchi Hall in Kitwe.

Dr. Wayne Myers, a missionary to Mexico and a long-time friend of CFNI, flew half way around the world to speak at the first Victory Bible College graduation a year later. Brother Myers' foresight amazed Nevers:

> *He (Wayne Myers) got so excited. I was embarrassed that there were only four students. But Brother Myers came and shook my hand and said, "Nevers, you are a man of faith." I said, "Say that again!" I didn't know what all the excitement was about. I had four students that I had taught in the back yard of my house all that I had learned back in Bible college in Dallas. Myers said, "You have really impressed me because you have invested your life in these four young people. Now you are producing leadership." He went back to Dallas and said that I was doing a mighty work of God.*[10]

Sister Lindsay later contacted Nevers and encouraged him to keep training nationals for full-time Christian service. In 1989 she

[10]Nevers Mumba, *Ibid*, 33.

assisted Nevers with the amazing acquisition of a 15-hectare (60-acre) farm, complete with 13 buildings, on the Kafue River in Kitwe. (The campus has a unique entrance. The only access to the land is by cable car across the crocodile-and-hippopotamus-infested water.) By faith, Victory Ministries purchased the farm in early 1989 for $130,000 under two stringent conditions. VM had to put a deposit of $30,000 down, and pay the balance by year end. Sister Lindsay presented the project in CFN's January magazine, while Nevers came over to the USA later in the year to raise the balance. The entire amount came in before 31 December and the Victory Institute of Biblical Studies (VIBS) has been training students from Zambia and surrounding countries ever since.

Like Wayne Myers, Reinhard admonished Nevers in the early years to **. . . not despise the day of small things** (Zechariah 4:10). CFAN purchased a new Toyota Land Cruiser for Nevers' crusade team in 1985. Half a dozen years later, Bonnke donated money to Victory Ministries to help them purchase a mobile sound system capable of reaching upwards of 20,000 people. This sound system is still used regularly today. Since meeting Nevers in 1981, Reinhard has done much to help Nevers' ministry flourish in Zambia. When Nevers would write his first book, *Integrity With Fire*, in 1994, Reinhard willingly agreed to write the foreword.

Nevers and Florence were busy in other ways. Shume-ol, their first child, a son, was born precisely nine months after their wedding day while daughter Tehillah came thirteen months after Shume-ol. Yehoshua, Micael and Natasha followed like dominoes. The Lord had given Nevers and Florence five beautiful children in seven quick years. Nevers facetiously calls this virility "the African Anointing." He once told the story of his children before preaching in an American church. As always, after the message he invited the sick to come forward for prayer and the laying on of hands. As Nevers moved down the prayer line, a woman respectfully asked that he pray for her without placing his hands on her head. When he asked her why, she replied that she did not want to get pregnant.

In addition to the Bible school and fledgling crusade ministry, Nevers and Florence planted Kitwe's Victory Bible Church in 1987. In ten years the congregation grew to 1,000. Since its inception, the Kitwe congregation willingly accepted the frequent absence of their pastor, who regularly held evangelistic crusades throughout Zambia's nine provinces, the rest of Africa, Europe, the Middle East,

Asia, South and North America. Both the leadership and the congregation were comfortable with this arrangement. Lubuto Nsofu rose from the Kitwe congregation to become Nevers' Associate Pastor. Pastor Nsofu and Florence would do the preaching in Nevers' absence.

Things had started small for Victory Ministries, but it didn't take long before things became huge. Nobody in Zambia had heard of Nevers Sekwila Mumba in 1984, but ten years later he would be a household name.

5

ZNBC

How did this Zambian preacher accomplish such a meteoric rise from obscurity to ubiquity? He went on television. Nevers initiated the first national Christian television broadcast, called *Zambia Shall Be Saved*. It was unheard of that a Zambian preacher would go on national TV, but that is exactly what Mumba did in 1989. The nation offered only one channel at that time, the Zambia National Broadcast Corporation (ZNBC), a government owned and operated station, reaching 1–2 million of Zambia's total population of 8 million. Mumba's one-hour weekly program aired on Sundays at 15:00 hours (3 PM). Thousands upon thousands watched this Bemba boy from Chinsali preach and pray for the sick. Testimonies of healing and miracles appeared recurrently on the program causing hundreds of needy viewers to call in regularly for prayer. *Zambia Shall Be Saved* rapidly became one of the most popular television programs in the country. It would be difficult to overstate the show's influence in the nation. Its popularity astonished a number of critics who thought this "son of the soil" should not tamper with worldly television.

An editor with the Weekly Post penned this sardonic commentary about Nevers:

> *With his unmatched eloquence and charismatic style, coupled with the public relations skills of his wife, Mumba soon became the country's most revered fundamentalist preacher. His meteoric rise came as a surprise to other, more established preachers. 'I went out of the country for a little while, and when I returned, Nevers Mumba was a big name in the country,' Youth and Sports Deputy minister, Reverend Peter —— remembers.*

The acrimony continues:

> *He (Nevers) hobnobbed with politicians, dazzled us on television, and hypnotised thousands with his fire and brimstone style.... James —— described Mumba as, 'A straightforward hypocrite who should be ashamed of himself for presenting such a meaningless programme on television....'*
>
> *It is not only Mumba's message that Pastor Franklin —— finds misplaced. The medium, too, is inappropriate, he says. 'If I wanted to save souls, I wouldn't go on television. I would go out in the shanties and the streets, where the people are....'*
>
> *'I suspect that pastor Mumba and his ministry are simply trying to use unsuspecting souls to earn a living,' Chingola resident Jeff —— said in 'The Times' recently.*

No phone calls. Plenty of perspiration.

The program's popularity and influence ambushed everyone at VM. Raising the money to keep *Zambia Shall Be Saved* on the air became a colossal challenge for the Victory team. Often called "the best-dressed man in Zambia," Nevers has always possessed a penchant for quality and his TV show reflected that. Pastor Mumba resisted the temptation to reduce the quality or the frequency of the broadcasts, but Victory Ministries soon had a large bill at ZNBC. One of the western ideas Nevers used to raise support was to host a live telethon at the ZNBC studio in Lusaka. The problem was that Zambians had never seen a telethon before. Would people respond? This gamble would either pay the ministry's bill or sink them deeper in debt. Nevers and his team were petrified as they prepared to go on live television. For the first twenty-five minutes of the broadcast, everything was eerily silent. No phone calls. Plenty of perspiration. Then, like a tidal wave, calls came in from across Zambia, pledging their financial support. People living within Lusaka walked or drove to ZNBC to personally deliver their cheques. Nevers' venture of faith had paid off handsomely; Victory's bill was cleared with Kwacha left over. It was even more amazing when one considers the average monthly income in Zambia is under $300.

During this period Nevers frequented the United States to raise money for the other challenges facing VM. Developing this large a ministry in a third world country simply required outside financial assistance. Nevers usually arrived in New York, but would spend most of his time in the Dallas/Fort Worth area. He was in Dallas so often that Mrs. Freda Lindsay let him use an apartment on the CFNI campus, which the Mumbas and other visiting Zambians still use today. Beginning with the graduation banquet in 1986 and continuing to the present, Sister Lindsay has Nevers speak to the CFNI student body whenever possible.

—

After graduating from CFNI in 1984, Heidi and I became the High School Pastors at Trinity Church in Cedar Hill, Texas, where we served for eight years. Since we lived only 15 minutes south of CFNI, Heidi and I saw Nevers once or twice a year. This frequent contact helped nurture the David-Jonathan friendship he and I had developed while Bible school students. On some trips to the US, Nevers traveled alone, while on others he brought Florence and a nursing child. I recall one spring visit when Nevers brought Denson Chipasha, who was the VM crusade coordinator and who later ran their international office from Windhoek, Namibia.

In the late 1980s Delta Airlines offered foreigners visiting America a thirty-day pass, good for unlimited, stand-by air travel anywhere in the contiguous United States. Nevers would purchase the Delta pass in London and then hit the ground running in New York. Delta later stopped offering that air-pass and I told Nevers it was because of him. Nevers could not get a credit card then, so renting an automobile was virtually impossible. Hence, it fell my lot on countless occasions to take him to and from the Dallas/Fort Worth airport. Although our friendship has revolved around airports, we have never flown together.

In the early days, Nevers' preaching invitations were sparse. He would preach to my youth group in Cedar Hill on Wednesday nights and we would both rejoice with the $100 offering. "Help Nevers" has been something God has asked me to do ever since I gave him my Adidas shoes in 1982. Therefore, I encouraged any and every pastor I knew to have Nevers in their pulpit. He soon preached the Sunday services at my church and for pastor-friends of mine, including Buddy Flowers and Roger Lewis in Austin, Texas, Irby McKnight in Sherman, Texas and Fred Bennett in Memphis, Tennessee. My pastor in Cedar Hill had graduated from

Oral Roberts University and had been friends with Carlton Pearson, so Nevers was soon preaching at Tulsa's Higher Dimensions Church for Carlton. Nevers and Florence loved to attend Carlton's Azusa Conference at Tulsa's Mabee Center and Carlton returned the favour by ministering in Zambia for Nevers in 1991 and 1995. Nevers made his own contacts as well. Every year around Easter Nevers would come to the States. Each returning year his itinerary was fuller. The offerings for his ministry also increased. Below is Nevers' Spring 1995 North American itinerary:

March 26	Agape Community Church, Colorado Springs, CO
March 27–31	Prophetic Ministries Conference, Colorado Springs, CO
Apr. 02	World Harvest Church, St. Catharines, ON
Apr. 05	Victory Church, Lethbridge, AB
Apr. 07	Victory Church, Medicine Hat, AB
Apr. 09	Ambassadors for Christ Church, Bertram, TX
Apr. 12–14	Booneville Christian Center, Booneville, AR
Apr. 16	Believer's Fellowship, Pewaukee, WI
Apr. 23–25	Harvest Time Church, Sherman, TX
Apr. 26–27	Steppingstone Church, Burleson, TX
Apr. 30–May 3	Word Fellowship, Harrisburg, PN
May 07	New St. Paul Tabernacle, Detroit, MI
May 12–14	Gillette Christian Center, Gillette, WY
May 21	Agape World Outreach Center, Virginia Beach, VA.

Nevers likes Kentucky Fried Chicken. Often after a service he would ask me to go through a KFC drive-thru to get some chicken and then we would drive either to my home or his CFNI apartment where we would talk for hours. Nevers would captivate me with faith-building stories of their crusades and TV ministry and the ever-present challenges that accompany such endeavors. Although we never made an international phone call to each other until mid-1993, and only saw each other once or twice a year in Dallas, our friendship would pick up right where it left off from the last visit. It was like we were never apart. Our friendship has possessed that unique quality for eighteen rewarding years.

Nevers invited me repeatedly to come see his country and though I craved to see Zambia in person, this did not come to pass until after my family and I had moved back to western Canada in late 1993.

Of Nevers' countless trips to Dallas, the one that stands out most in my mind occurred in early October 1991. Since he had already been to the States that spring and didn't mention a return visit in the fall, I knew that something unusual must have occurred. Nevers and I met as usual in terminal 4E at the airport. We made small talk at the carousel waiting for his luggage to come out. He had bad news and good news. Nevers usually has a large black briefcase with wheels as his carry-on but this time he had a gym bag. As he was obviously tired from the jet lag, I offered to carry his gym bag, but when I went to pick it up I could barely get it off the ground. "What is in here?" I asked. Nevers whispered, "I'll tell you later." Next came the suitcases. One was normal weight while the other seemed to be lined with lead. It took both of us to get the heavy suitcase off of the carousel and onto the cart, grunting all the way.

> ***. . . Nevers explained to me why his luggage weighed a ton.***

When we finally got into my car and were headed south down Highway 360, Nevers explained to me why his luggage weighed a ton. At their recent Lusaka crusade, Victory Ministries had blown all four of their new speakers. Victory's technical crew had then taken the mammoth speakers apart and removed the fried hardware. Hoping the sound engineer in DeSoto, Texas who built Victory's system would cover the repair under warranty, Nevers had lugged the "guts" of these speakers all the way from Zambia, two in the carry-on and two in one suitcase. Understandably, the engineer took one look at the cooked wiring and told Nevers the damage was clearly the result of human error and not faulty equipment. It cost Nevers $3,000 to replace the hardware.

That was the bad news. The good news came from his report on their two recent Lusaka crusades. Reinhard and Nevers had met recently in Bonnke's home in Frankfurt. When asked by Reinhard about VM's crusade attendance, Nevers replied, "Between 1,000 to 2,000." Pastor Bonnke then pronounced, "Gone are the days of 1,000 to 2,000. Your meetings will now attract crowds of 10,000 to 20,000." Victory Ministries crusade attendance had been swelling just as Bonnke had predicted.

The VM crusade team had previously avoided the haughty capital city of Lusaka with its one million inhabitants, fearing the meetings would be ridiculed and the results meager. However, Nevers has never been one to step down from a challenge. A crusade in Lusaka was providentially planned for September 1990. Unrest permeated the nation that year as Zambians from every province demanded multi-party elections. Dr. Kenneth David Kaunda (respectfully referred to as "KK" by Zambians) and his Freedom Fighters had broken the chains of British colonialism off of the Zambian people, emancipating the nation on 24 October 1964. They promptly changed the name of their country from Northern Rhodesia to Zambia. President Kaunda and his socialist-leaning United National Independence Party, or UNIP (a party he started in 1960), had been in charge ever since. The Zambian people were indebted to KK as their Father and Founding Head of State, but after 26 years they clearly desired a democratic voice in selecting Zambia's leader.

Previous Zambian "elections" used humorously simple ballots. Zambian citizens, many of whom are illiterate, were instructed to check the picture of the garden hoe if they wanted KK and his UNIP to stay in power. If not, they were to check the picture of the frog. That the frog represented nothing was never explained to the voter.

The 1990 unrest in Zambia was indicative of a global trend. The Iron Curtain had come down the year before, creating a ripple effect around the world. Totalitarian governments, like East Germany, were either imploding or acceding to democratic reforms. Would UNIP follow the trend of other prudent left-wing governments shifting right or would they unwisely enforce their one-party rule, leading possibly to civil war? Ostensibly, President Kaunda was not open to democratic reforms, fostering food riots in the capital city.

In spite of the escalating tension, the Victory Ministries crusade team planned their first major Lusaka crusade in Woodlands Stadium that September. Nevers was determined to show the citizens of Lusaka that their hope must be in the God of Zambia and not in its government. Momentum was building as the nightly crowds approached 10,000. Victory Ministry's crusade was having a definite, positive impact in the tense capital. In fact, President Kaunda had been following the Lusaka meetings and sent word to Nevers that the latter's presence was requested at State House on Independence Avenue.

A call came in telling me I had to be at the State House at 8:00 the next morning. One of my associates (Jeston Katebe) drove with me to meet the President for the first time — officially. We were welcomed warmly by everyone and were whisked into a waiting room. On the way we silently asked God for supernatural wisdom. When we were called in, the thick double doors were closed behind us, and President Kaunda stretched his hand out to greet us. After we were seated, God's miracle began. The anointing of God came upon me and I could feel it. As I studied the President I saw that he looked thin and weary. Things were taking their toll on him and it was showing. At the height of the opposition he was facing, I saw he was a lonely man. Breaking the short silence, he started by saying, "I've been wanting to meet with you since you began the crusade early this week, but I have been extremely busy." Looking at him I knew he wanted to be open and freely share his hurts and fears, so I began with what God had given me early that morning during my prayer time. It was the story of the "Rich Young Ruler."

I responded to him by saying, "Sir, God is not able to help you until you surrender your life and give up any fetishes that could be around the State House." I dealt with his involvement in Eastern religions. My reply was based on Mark 10:17–21, which reads,

And when he was gone forth into the way, there came one running, and kneeled to him, and asked him, Good Master, what shall I do that I may inherit eternal life? And Jesus said unto him, Why callest thou me good? There is none good but one, that is, God. Thou knowest the commandments, Do not commit adultery, Do not kill, Do not steal, Do not bear false witness, Defraud not, Honour thy father and mother.

And he answered and said unto him, Master, all these have I observed from my youth. Then Jesus beholding him loved him, and said unto him, One thing thou lackest: go thy way, sell whatsoever thou hast, and give to the poor, and thou shalt have treasure in heaven: and come, take up the cross, and follow me.

Jesus said to the rich young ruler, "One thing thou lackest." I said to the President, "Jesus will help you by saving you from your sins. You have to give up your faith in other gods and trust only Jesus for salvation." An altar call was made and the response was immediate. The President climbed down from his seat and knelt down in front of me to honour and receive Jesus Christ into his heart. We joined hands and had a glorious time of prayer. He repeated the sinner's prayer after me just like in the crusades. My associate was watching all this, amazed at my boldness and the President's response, and the presence of the Holy Spirit in the room. Little did I know that in two hours time the President was going to address the nation on radio and television to diffuse a political time bomb, one that could have brought untold bloodshed to Zambia. He (Kaunda) declared Zambia a multi-party state.[11]

I got goose bumps when Nevers told me this story. It reminded me of the Old Testament days when a godly king would seek the counsel of the prophet before making a major decision.

Kaunda set the election date for 31 October 1991 and referred to the nation now as The Third Republic of Zambia.[12] Hence, it was but a couple of weeks before the election when Nevers came to Dallas with the speaker hardware.

While UNIP had the obvious advantage of 26 years of organisation, a plethora of new political parties sprung up overnight as the Zambian people cherished their new-found democratic freedom.

Frederick Titus Jacob Chiluba, an intelligent, diminutive man ascended from the throng to become the serious opponent to President Kaunda. Chiluba, a labour union leader, had previously been detained in prison by the UNIP government for publicly speaking out against Zambia's Marxist government. During his incarceration he found Christ and was later filled with the Holy Spirit at a CFAN crusade. Chiluba joined the Movement for Multi-Party Democracy, or MMD, winning the party nomination on 1 March 1991 with 63% of the vote. He promised Zambians swift democratic reforms, including a liberalised economy. Chiluba won the Halloween 1991 national election handily, carrying approximately 80% of the popular vote to become only the second president in Zambia's 27-year history.

The New York Times News Service had this to say about the 1991 election:

After food riots last year and the emergence of Mr. Chiluba's party as a credible challenge, Mr. Kaunda legalized opposition parties last December. That action set in motion Thursday's election, which

[11]Nevers Mumba, *Ibid*, 40–42.

[12]The First Republic refers to the infant years of the country, while the Second Republic points to the one-party rule of the UNIP.

international observers and diplomats said was being watched by other one-party states in Africa.[13]

—

The late 1980s and early 1990s had been a time of breakthroughs for VM: a debt-free Victory Bible College campus, regional crusades with unheard-of crowds, Victory Bible Church in Kitwe, new Victory Churches being spawned across the nation, and the *Zambia Shall Be Saved* national television program. Victory Ministries printed Pastor Mumba's feverish six-month itinerary in their 1992 newsletter:

June 14 – 23	Amsterdam Crusade
June 27 – July 1	Suriname Crusade (South America)
July 4	Ndola Dinner
July 10	Monze Dinner
July 11	Livingstone Dinner
July 15 – 17	Guyana Crusade
July 28 – Aug. 1	Cameroon Minister's Conference
Aug. 9 – 16	Celebration and Crusade (later called "International Conference")
Sept. 19 – 26	Lusaka Crusade (see journal entries)
Sept. 26	Lusaka Dinner
Oct. 10 – 17	Harare Crusade (Zimbabwe)
Nov. 7 – 14	Israel Tour
Nov. 27 – 30	Windhoek Crusade (Namibia)

This rapid ministry growth had been hard on Florence and their young family. The Mumbas moved fourteen times in the first five years of their marriage. Nevers was gone more than he was home; the words "relax" and "vacation" were not in Nevers' vocabulary from 1984–1994. Florence used to cry often, but when she realised Nevers did not see the tears, she stopped crying. She is naturally easy-going, but her husband's intensity, coupled with his frequent absences, forced her out of her shell, making her the more assertive and independent person she is today.

The affable Florence would regularly prepare larger portions for the "unexpected" and hungry VM team members Nevers would bring home for supper. Other meals went cold as Nevers would

[13]New York Times News Service, *Dallas Morning News Archives*, 01 November 1991.

come home, change clothes and announce on his way out that he and his team were fasting and praying to prepare themselves for the next crusade. The last two Mumba children, Micael and Natasha, came early while Dad was away preaching in crusades outside Zambia. Florence told Nevers that his idea of having twelve children was implausible and she was not having any more children. The number stopped at five.

> ***. . .before she knew it, Shalom Christian School had started.***

Since she found schools within Kitwe inadequate, Florence started home-schooling her children. Other parents asked if they could have their children in her school and before she knew it, Shalom Christian School had started.

The Lord saw Florence's sacrifices and blessed her and her young family with an amazing miracle. A wealthy widow attended a Pentecostal church in Kitwe. Having worked previously in Europe, she desired to spend her golden years in Cyprus. On the odd occasion she permitted Victory Ministries to film excerpts of *Zambia Shall Be Saved* in her palatial estate on Jambo Drive. This is how she met Nevers and Florence Mumba.

While preparing to move to Cyprus, she met with her pastor for counsel and told him that instead of selling her $200,000 home, she would like to give it to the young Mumba family. Her pastor concurred wholeheartedly, making the Mumbas the surprised new owners of one of the most elegant homes in Kitwe. The timing was perfect. Enrolment at Shalom Christian School was blossoming so the new house doubled temporarily as a school. Soon the school outgrew the house so Florence had to relocate her school, several times, within Kitwe.

—

For reasons I have never completely understood, Nevers keeps his thoughts carefully locked in the vault of his heart. People who sit mesmerised by Pastor Mumba's preaching and then meet him in private afterwards are often surprised to discover that Nevers is rather bashful. He is a quiet person who enjoys solitude. To those close to him, he chooses to communicate his wishes indirectly, which can be exasperating. Reading his much-guarded journal is the only way to really understand what is going on inside Nevers, but the only people brazen enough to attempt such a breach of privacy are Florence and me. After much prodding, here are approved (and sadly clinical) excerpts from Nevers' diary during the 1991 and 1992 Lusaka crusades:

> Saturday, September 21, 1991: First day of the crusade, had more than six thousand people — a massive altar call — commissioned and dedicated the new PA system — ZNBC filmed the service. Beginning message "Where Are You?"
>
> Sunday, September 22, 1991: Better crowd than yesterday - preached with an interpreter — a wonderful anointing toward the end. My Mother greeted people on the platform. My family came. Message "Take Me to Jesus."
>
> Monday, September 23, 1991: Prayer meeting with the team. Refreshing and encouraging... Preached without interpreter — the Word came out clear and distinct. Had so many sickly people brought for prayer.
>
> Sunday, September 20, 1992: Started day with prayer and 70 press-ups. Preached at Chiluba's church on "Now is the Time." Had an offering of K12,000. Had a short rest then preached at crusade "When Jesus Calls." A good start. My Mother in attendance.
>
> Tuesday, September 22, 1992: Day of the Holy Spirit — enjoyed my times of prayer today — felt God real close to me — had a good team prayer meeting and Bible study. The best service so far, spoke on "Overcoming the Spirit of the World." Great response to the altar. Thank-you Lord.
>
> Wednesday, September 23, 1992: Woke up exhausted physically but enjoyed a continuous flow of God's Spirit...
>
> Thursday, September 24, 1992: ...A great day of expectancy. Crusade began to pick up a spiritual momentum. Preached on "The Power of the Blood." Flowed well with a tremendous response to salvation — even before I made the altar call, many people began to walk forward. Tremendous presence of the Holy Ghost.

—

Nevers' riveting sermons, whether viewed on ZNBC or seen in person at one of his crusades, had elevated him to religious prominence in the nation. Media pundits, delighted by, or disgusted with, Pastor Mumba, referred to him by his first name. Saying "Nevers" will produce a reaction in Zambia. His well-publicised State House invitations from Kenneth Kaunda and later Frederick Chiluba showed that Pastor Mumba was also well connected politically.

Unfortunately, Nevers was about to find out the hard way that mixing religion and politics is like combining baking soda and vinegar: eruptions are inevitable.

ZAMBIA'S POLITICIAN

. . . but do I have enough politician in me to be a preacher?

Nevers, with the sign "Only Jesus Fills Emptiness," at *The Who* concert, December 1982.

The nervous Nevers, in his light green suit, picks up his fiancée at the Dallas airport, January 1984.

Double-dating at the Dallas Zoo, January 1984.

The two soon-to-be preachers, clad in navy, May 1984.

Florence with Nevers at his graduation, 13 May 1984.

The Mumba's wedding picture, 13 April 1985.

The first four graduates from Victory Bible College in Zambia. From left to right: Lazarus Myila, Jeston Katebe, Jefferson Sichangwa and Gamaliel Mwanza.

This photo of Nevers in front of one of the Bible School buildings (formerly a squash court), comes from the CFN fund-raising appeal. The caption reads, "Begin 1989 by giving your first gift to missions!"

Florence, Nevers holding baby Yehoshua, Heidi holding baby Courtney, Me holding Nathanael. Spring 1989.

A rare picture of Nevers vacationing with his family in South Africa, early 1990s.

Victory International Conference, August 1993 at Mulungushi Centre. From left to right on the front row are Eva Sanderson, Reinhard Bonnke, Nevers Mumba, President and Mrs. Chiluba and Lubuto Nsofu.

Nevers introducing President Chiluba to Ghana's Mensa Otabil. Lubuto Nsofu is on the right.

The President and the Pastor visit the VIP lounge before entering the Mulungushi auditorium. Nevers looks distracted.

Another first for Nevers. Zambia's historical relationship with Israel has been cool. Nevers tried to improve that by leading trips to the Holy Land. He is in the centre back.

Victory International Conference, 10 August 1995 at Mulungushi. I took this photo and it remains one of my favorite for it capsulises what Nevers is all about. He has just finished preaching to a packed crowd and has made the altar call. Hundreds have responded and their hunger for God is apparent.

Nevers at his office on the Bible School campus.

Another picture of the two of us dressing together. This photo was taken at the entry way to his house. We were on our way to church, December 1996.

My daughter Courtney, Heidi, Florence and Pauline Musonda in Canada, October 1997. We all decided to dress in African garb.

Shume-ol, Tehillah, Nathanael, Yehoshua, Micael and Natasha in the Mumba's yard, December 1997.

Dr. Mumba leaving the 4 September 1997 press conference. He has just announced the formation of the National Christian Coalition (NCC).

I chose this photo for two reasons. First, this is the only photo I have ever seen of Nevers with Kenneth Kaunda. Secondly, I had no idea I was going to meet KK at his home that day, 12 August 1999. Notice his ever-present white handkerchief of peace.

6

A CHRISTIAN NATION

When the righteous are in authority, the people rejoice: but when the wicked beareth rule, the people mourn (Proverbs 29:2).

Upon being sworn in as Zambia's second president in late 1991, Frederick Chiluba quickly renounced corruption in government and declared Zambia a Christian nation. He even went so far as to have this declaration enshrined into the national constitution. This was an ambitious goal for Chiluba, as government-corruption is often sadly and inextricably meshed into the polity of the dark continent.

Chiluba announced that prominent church ministers would be granted a diplomatic passport since they were the ambassadors of the Christian nation. Nevers gratefully received his special passport from President Chiluba in November, 1992.

President Chiluba and Pastor Mumba swiftly became friends. They met at State House just twenty-one days after Chiluba moved in. Nevers described their first meeting:

> *What a difference it made to meet a man who was not just the president, but a brother in the Lord, too. When we met, he (Chiluba) stretched out his hands and shouted, "Brother Nevers." We spent time together over lunch, and in the evening we shared from God's Word. It was rich. Oh, what joy I felt to see a president pray in the Spirit with me . . . .*[14]

The President invited Pastor Mumba, among others, to address Christians and government officials at the Mulungushi Centre on 29 December 1994. The President asked the speakers to address the declaration of Zambia being a Christian nation. Reciprocating the

[14]Nevers Mumba, *Ibid*, 42.

favour, President Chiluba agreed to address the delegates at Victory Ministries International Conference, held annually at the Mulungushi Centre in Lusaka.

As one of the 1995 International Conference speakers, it was an unforgettable privilege for me not only to witness Zambia's new president addressing the 5,000 delegates crammed into the hall on that Tuesday night in early August, but also to have lunch with President Chiluba and a group of distinguished guests, earlier that day at Plot One. As the President spoke in front of his people at the conference and to the nation via live television, my traveling companion Mervyn Mediwake and I couldn't help but notice how pastoral Chiluba appeared. The President even referred to himself as Pastor Chiluba and read confidently from Genesis 4. He discussed serious theology, reflecting a keen intellect. After speaking, his aides wanted the President off the stage and into the waiting motorcade as streets all over the capital had been blocked for security. Their plan was to hustle the President back to State House as soon as he finished his greeting. More than once however, Chiluba waved off the security and remained on the platform, listening to the preaching of Carlton Pearson. (It was at this very service that African-American Pastor Kingsley Fletcher surprised everyone by presenting Nevers with an honorary doctorate from the Full Gospel Christian Theological Seminary in Flint, Michigan for Nevers' outstanding gospel work in Zambia.)

President Chiluba's wife, Vera, already a friend of Florence's family, enjoyed visiting with the Mumbas on the phone and in person. On one such memorable occasion, Mrs. Chiluba's advance team called the Mumba residence unexpectedly and informed them that the President's wife would be at their home in ten minutes. Nevers took the call as Florence was not home. He quickly went into panic mode, cleaning up the children while the house workers tidied up. Mrs. Chiluba arrived on time, visited briefly with Nevers and the children, and then kindly left a State House tumbler as a token of her surprise visit.

Only months into the MMD's administration, a mysterious tragedy faced the new president. Zambia's national football (soccer) team showed promise of making it to the 1994 World Cup. Football is like religion in Zambia, so the whole nation cheered on their young team as they traveled on 28 April 1993 for a match against Gabon. Tragically, the Zambian military jet transporting the team crashed on route, leaving no survivors. The entire nation went into shock. At the massive funeral President Chiluba wept openly, spawning spontaneous mourning among the thousands in attendance. It seemed that when the President cried, he gave permission for the nation to cry. This funeral is one of the most moving pieces of video footage to ever come out of Zambia.

—

For the first fifteen years of our friendship, "www." meant nothing, so I craved any news out of Zambia. The fatal plane crash of the soccer team was only the third time between 1984 and 1995 that Zambia made news in the West. The first time occurred in the late 1980s when Peter Jennings, the anchor for ABC World News Tonight, spent a total of ten seconds announcing a flood in Zambia. A letter to Nevers from me was in the mail the next day asking if everything was okay. He wrote back, thanking me for the information, as he had not heard of any flooding in his nation. He had then checked into it and discovered there was indeed flooding in the Eastern province. That Nevers was unaware of this flood really surprised me, for he habitually watches, reads, or listens to, the daily news.

02 November 1992 placed Zambia in the western press the second time when the Dallas Morning News announced FTJ Chiluba's landslide election victory. The story explained how former U.S. President Jimmy Carter and his organization were invited by the Zambian government to observe the election, Carter being present to affirm the accuracy and integrity of the proceedings. I clipped out the article from the Texas newspaper and sent it to Nevers.

> *Mr. Chiluba's overwhelming victory in what international monitors called a "free and fair" election will be a sharp setback for one-party countries and a big boost for democracy in Africa, said former President Jimmy Carter. "What happens in Zambia will set an example for Africa," said Mr. Carter, who headed a group of international observers of the elections for president and Parliament held Thursday.*[15]

[15]Detroit Free Press, *Dallas Morning News Archives*, 02 Nov. 1991.

Since African elections are too often contaminated with corruption, the American government was elated to see the germination of honest democracy in Marxist Zambia.

In spite of the landslide defeat, Dr. Kenneth David Kaunda stepped down gracefully, reflecting the stellar statesman he truly is. After 27 years, "the Old Man," as Zambians affectionately call their Founding Father, stepped aside with dignity. KK and his Freedom Fighters had successfully snapped the colonial chains not only off of Northern Rhodesia but also off of several other African countries. History will be kind to Kaunda, recognising him as one of the great African statesman during the last half of the 20th century.

To ensure that Zambia would never return to autocratic rule, President Chiluba and his MMD government set in a two-term limit on any Zambian president, similar to the restriction enshrined in the United States Constitution. The only difference between Zambia and the United States was the length of terms, the former using a five year term, the latter four. Therefore, Chiluba was but a year away from his second election when I made my first trip to Zambia in August 1995. His first term had gone okay. Unfortunately, the same could not be said of the second. Controversy doggedly pursued and eventually overwhelmed the nation's second president.

7

CAPTAIN SOLO

While in his first term, "FTJ," as the Zambian media referred to their President, passed an amendment in parliament, placing even tighter restrictions on future presidents. Identical to the US Constitution, any president of Zambia must be a Zambian citizen. The MMD presented another bill requesting that not only must any future president be a Zambian citizen, his parents must be also. This amendment appeared to be a direct vendetta against Dr. Kaunda whose parents had been missionaries from neighbouring Malawi. KK had not voiced his intentions regarding the 1996 election, but this clause was ostensibly created to close the door on any opportunity for Kaunda to return to the national scene. The charge against Kaunda by some of the irrational MMD leaders was ludicrous and laughable: KK had illegally masqueraded as a Zambian to assume the presidency of the first Republic. KK and his UNIP leaders cried foul, as did the free press in Zambia. Some UNIP candidates protested further by boycotting the 1996 federal election.

Determined reporters from the non-government-run media began making credible claims that President Chiluba's parents were not from Zambia either, but rather from the Democratic Republic of Congo (or DRC, formerly Zaire). While the government decision against Kaunda came swiftly, the ruling on Chiluba's genealogy has yet to be delivered. (Both of Nevers Mumba's parents are Zambians. Dr. Mumba hails from a family whose Chinsali parents were close associates to the Kaundas and Kapwepwes. Nevers' deceased father, Sunday Peter Sekwila Mumba was 'Old Lion' Harry Mwaanga Nkumbula's classmate at Chalimbana Teachers' College in 1943 and was one of the topmost heroes of Zambia's fight against British colonialism. Nevers' Mother, Maritha Mpango Mumba, was born in 1922, and with 12 children and 55 grandchildren to her credit, is still very much alive, residing within Lusaka.)

In 1991 Jimmy Carter hailed Zambia as a champion of African democracy, but it appeared to have digressed back to African abuse in 1996. All this in a Christian nation. President Frederick T. J. Chiluba was re-elected in the disputed national election of 1996. The final results were distorted by the boycott, making the final count less than significant.

Controversial rumours began cropping up about the 1993 air disaster in Gabon. The football players had been assigned a military jet rather than a commercial air liner. Why? The reports out of Gabon insinuated the Zambian military jet had not requested clearance to enter Gabonese air space. Thus, the Gabonese defense system viewed the aircraft as a threat to national security and subsequently shot it down. The Zambian Government promised their citizens a full chronicle on the disaster. At present, the nation is still waiting.

Before Chiluba came into power, hard currency could be brought into Zambia but not out. This was one of the many down sides of the closed economy he inherited in 1991. Unfortunately, there would also be a down side for the MMD's promised immediate liberalisation of Zambia's closed economy. Similar to nations like Russia with closed market economies that became open over night, Zambia suffered some of the highest inflation on the planet in the 1990s. Goods were becoming more available in Zambia, but were too expensive for the average worker. I witnessed this first-hand during my second visit to Kitwe in December, 1996 when a store had a new 21-inch Sony TV "on sale" for K2,000,000 ($450).

Zambians burgeoning disappointment with their ruling government was symbolised by the 28 October 1997 quasi-coup attempt by a motley crew of drunken military men, led by Steven Lungu, who claimed to be "Captain Solo." The coup occurred four short days after Zambia's 33rd anniversary as a free nation. Shortly after 6 AM, Zambians woke up to what many later described as a slurred, drunken-sounding voice announcing the overthrow of the government over the national radio station, ZNBC. Captain Lungu claimed to speak on behalf of a "national redemption council" who were "saving our nation from total collapse." He demanded, among other things, the immediate suspension of the constitution and the resignation of President Chiluba by 9 AM.

While a smattering of soldiers in armoured cars captured the radio station, another small band of soldiers attempted to take Zambian army commander Lieutenant General Nobby Simbeye hostage. Their attempt failed. By 8 AM, ZNBC radio was silent and at 8:36 AM a lieutenant colonel announced to the nation over the radio that the government was in control. A ZNBC crew later broadcast the image of Captain Steven Lungu lying on the ground as soldiers stomped on his chest.

Citing Section 30 of the Zambian constitution, President Chiluba declared a state of emergency, placing the country under military rule.

The MMD government initially did not place any blame on opposition parties, for at no time in "Captain Solo's" radio address did he mention Kenneth Kaunda, UNIP, or any other political leader or party. The coup appeared to be the sole idea of Lungu and a handful of comrades.

Surprisingly, the state of emergency stayed on longer than seemed necessary.

> *"The government is not suspicious that the opposition was behind the attempted coup," presidential spokesman Richard Sakala told reporters at a 29 October news briefing that was held while President Chiluba met with his cabinet.*[16]

Surprisingly, the state of emergency stayed on longer than seemed necessary. Human rights organisations, including Amnesty International, began to speak up suggesting the coup attempt was being used by the ruling government to justify an unnecessary state of emergency, allowing them to suppress political activity under the premise of investigating the failed coup. Under military rule, any Zambian citizen can be detained for 28 days without charge. It is alleged that police officers tortured at least six of the over 100 people detained, coercing them to confess to the involvement of political activists in the coup. Several of these opposition activists were subsequently arrested and detained.

The growing rumours of human rights violations and torture proved to be true. One such case involved Dean Mung'omba, leader of the Zambia Democratic Congress (ZDC) party who had earlier accused Chiluba of vote-rigging the "not free and not fair" election of 1996. Mung'omba became the first political detainee on 31 October 1997 when eight police officers arrested him at his house and placed him under incommunicado detention at police headquarters in downtown Lusaka. Fifteen police officers tortured the

[16] Agence France Presse, wire service report, 29 October 1997.

ZDC leader for the next four days, demanding that he confess his guilt and implicate other opposition activists as co-conspirators. Though under unspeakable duress, Mung'omba continually denied his or any other political leader's association in the plot. His lawyers were not allowed to contact their client until he appeared in court on 4 November 1997, "bearing the marks of bruises and cigarette burns." Mung'omba would get his day in court:

> *Police interrogators allegedly suspended Dean Mung'omba from a metal bar by his handcuffed hands and rope-tied legs and beat him, in a method of torture. . . that is known as "the swing." Later that same day, Dean Mung'omba alleges he was tortured again, and that twice his police interrogators tried to make him implicate Kenneth Kaunda. Among the torture methods said to have been used were electrical shocks to his handcuffs and the application of burning cigarettes to his arms and legs. Mung'omba was also deprived of sleep, and starved of food and water for the first four days in custody.*[17]

To extend Mr. Mung'omba's 28-day detention, the President personally had to sign each extension, which he did. These extensions kept the innocent Mung'omba in prison. The torture continued while the pleas for clemency from Mung'omba's wife, appearing in the media, fell on deaf ears at State House. It seemed the MMD was using the ZDC president as an example of what happens to those who would dare speak out against the ruling government.

After speaking in the central city of Kabwe on 23 August 1997, Kenneth Kaunda and companion Roger Chongwe were ambushed in their Toyota Landcruiser by paramilitary soldiers. Chongwe had a bullet enter his cheek and exit his neck while KK's head was grazed from a sniper's bullet. Who was behind this assault? Kaunda spent the fall of 1997 recuperating in the United States. He returned home in December and was arrested on Christmas Day for his alleged involvement in the October coup. USA President Bill Clinton released a statement the next day condemning the arrest and detention of Kaunda, which Chiluba ignored. Hence, when Clinton toured southern Africa a few months later, he bypassed Zambia. Denied access to legal counsel, Kaunda was whisked away to a maximum security prison near Kabwe. He protested immediately by going on a hunger strike, which ended five days later at the urging of former Tanzanian president Julius Nyerere, who visited

[17]Affidavit by Dean Mung'omba to the High Court for Zambia, Principal Registry, Lusaka. 1997/HP/2617.

KK and insisted that "the Old Man" eat something. As 1998 dawned, President Chiluba moved Zambia's founding president back to Lusaka and placed KK and his wife, Betty, under strict house arrest at the Kaunda's Kulundu residence in Lusaka. Other than the coerced confessions of detainees, no evidence connecting the opposition leader to the coup was ever presented. Kaunda, who rarely appears in public without his white handkerchief of peace, appeared to have no connection to the coup, yet he and his spouse were also being mistreated by the MMD. This unjust persecution also caught the attention of international organisations, including the United Nations, who pressured Chiluba into removing the house arrest, which he did, in July.

Now Zambia was in the western news too often. Sadly, all of the coverage was negative.

Like Kaunda, Pastor Mumba was out of the country when the military coup was attempted. This seemed to be enough evidence to a handful of paranoid MMD leaders that the pastor was also attempting to topple the elected government. Double agents of Zambia's Special Branch covertly contacted Florence Mumba, warning her that Nevers should not say anything publicly when he returned home from Canada or he too might be detained. Florence thanked them and passed the warning onto Nevers. He returned home without incident. (Pastor Mumba was in my southern Alberta home when news of the coup reached him. He called home immediately and discovered that those involved had been arrested.)

What did the ruling president have to say regarding all that had transpired since 28 October 1997? In his speech opening parliament on 16 January 1998, President Chiluba told the House: "The fears and anxieties expressed by traditional nay-sayers regarding human rights violations during the state of emergency have proved unfounded. The state of emergency has not interfered with the normal daily lives or the fundamental freedoms and liberties of our people."

The disheveled attempt to overthrow the government was swiftly squelched, but not before news of it traveled around the world, adversely affecting foreign confidence.

The nation was still under a state of emergency when I made my third visit to Zambia in early December, 1997. Day-to-day living for most Zambians had not been affected. The only noticeable difference was the Lusaka airport, which was closed from dusk until dawn. Eight Canadians, including my wife and oldest son Nathanael, accompanied me on this trip that would include my first visit to Zambia's pristine South Luangwa Valley National Park. The virgin beauty of the park, coupled with the magnificently abundant African wildlife, made the viewing safari a truly once-in-a-lifetime experience for our team. Sadly, the owner/operators of the Chichele Lodge complained about steadily shrinking business due to neglected roads and the recent closure of the country's only international airline, Zambia Airways. I explained to the owners that few people in the West had ever heard of Zambia, never mind the South Luangwa Valley. Furthermore, if a failed coup attempt and a state of emergency are the only Zambian news items to reach the developed nations, Lodge owners could be assured that money-spending tourists would not be visiting their beautiful park.

President Chiluba's effort to liberalise the economy did produce some new foreign investment, which I can also affirm firsthand. A banker from Italy purchased the dilapidated Mfuwe Lodge from the Zambian Government and completely renovated it. The Lodge, located just inside Luangwa's southern entrance, re-opened in 1998 and is *the* place to stay for any tourist considering a trip to the South Luangwa Valley. Two Canadians, a father and son, joined me on my fourth trip to Zambia in August 1999 and we stayed at the new five-star Mfuwe Lodge. It is expensive, but worth every penny.

—

During Chiluba's first term, the President and the Pastor talked regularly on the phone. For security reasons, the phone number was changed every two weeks at the State House, making it extremely difficult for Pastor Mumba to return President Chiluba's calls. To solve this dilemma, the President gave his personal number, which is not routinely changed, to Nevers. In the early years the two talked often, met often and prayed often. By the second term however, their friendship had become icy. Contact from Vera Chiluba suddenly came to a halt, although Florence wondered if Mrs. Chiluba had any choice in the matter. The rumours leaking out of State House suggested the Chiluba's marriage was slowly disintegrating, due to growing infidelity. The President and his wife were seldom seen in public together.

The MMD's treatment of Mung'omba, Kaunda, the repressed Gabon air disaster report, the "renounced" but apparently persisting government embezzlement, which caused sporadic bank closures where the life savings of honest citizens evaporated overnight, were but a handful of the controversies that clouded the ruling party early in their second administration. The media went on the offensive, hoping to snare their scripture-quoting President. Nevers found himself in a conundrum. He sincerely wanted to support his Christian brother, FTJ Chiluba, but was growing alarmed by the blatant and hypocritical partisanship of the MMD. Should Nevers confront the President privately? Should he speak up in the media and let the nation know that the conduct of the ruling government was not consistent with their declaration of Zambia as a Christian nation?

What had begun as a dream for Zambian believers was turning into a nightmare.

8

THIS TURBULENT PRIEST

Seeing the precious gospel of Jesus Christ tarnished by government, Nevers initially admonished President Chiluba gently and privately via personal mail. Nevers wrote several letters to the President but doubted that FTJ received any of them. Finally, in 1999, the President wrote Nevers a brief letter acknowledging the receipt of a recent letter. 'Has the President read my previous letters?' Nevers wondered.

Mumba's next step was to publicly scrutinize, albeit carefully, the inconsistent conduct of the MMD party. At a 20 June 1998 press briefing at Kabwe's Elephant Head Hotel, Dr. Mumba explained his position:

> *It was not until I noticed the activities of government were going to become detrimental to the witness of Christ that I started to whisper some concerns to the Head of State. I was concerned about drug trafficking allegations that were being substantiated by both the local and international press. Names were given and evidence was available. The immorality of a number of Ministers further tarnished our image in the region, as did the intolerance to other political players, evidenced by visible hatred and insults. This conflict almost cost all of us, when on 28 October 1997 we experienced an attempted coup. The detentions of innocent people, torture and all that followed confirmed that the Christ we had mentioned was no longer involved in running the affairs of the nation. The manipulation of the 1996 constitution, the corrupted electoral process, the lack of transparency in the business of government officials, were all indicators that our MMD honeymoon had come to an end.*

Charles Kachikoti, writing the Times' "Campaign Trail" had this to say about Pastor Mumba's position:

Evangelists have never agreed about how to relate to politics and for this reason many will tend to ignore or despise whatever Dr. Nevers Mumba of Victory Ministries is accomplishing in trying to salt the Zambian politics.

For that reason, there are those evangelical leaders who are seen as being unhelpful to the republican president by agreeing, actively or passively, with the wrong-doing in Government.[18]

Mumba's comments produced a frigid response from the State House. Their message to Pastor Mumba came loud and clear; the gospel and politics should not mix. The paradox of the MMD position was too comical to be ignored; some of their cabinet ministers who criticised Mumba the harshest were themselves clergymen.

Nevers' political activity intensified greatly when he decided to form a new political organisation. Along with distinguished colleagues Florence Chola, Simattaa Simattaa, Emanuel Shikaputo and Eva Sanderson, Nevers created the National Christian Coalition, or NCC, on 04 September 1997, to conscientiously address the growing concerns in Zambian politics. This speech marked a water-shed day in Nevers' life. He started to cross the bridge.

INTRODUCTION

Our generation celebrates the rare privilege of being the generation that shall witness the turn of a century. Within three years, we shall enter the new millennium.

While other people consider all days the same; God has divided time into seasons. There are days, weeks, months, years and centuries. Each new day is meant to afford us with a new set of opportunities and challenges.

Africa, and in particular Zambia, has to take advantage of the change of seasons. We need to understand our spiritual, social, economic and political problems, and make a united resolve to reverse the trend in the next century. We must together refuse to enter the next century in weakness, but in resolve and confidence. It will be a highly competitive century, where the heavy weights will step upon the lightweights on the international stage.

[18]Charles Kachikoti, "Christianity Must Salt Politics" *Times of Zambia*, August 1996.

We therefore in Zambia need to carefully determine our course of action that shall bring total healing and emancipation to our society. We should refuse to be underdogs, underprivileged and underdeveloped. We must agree to set aside the great divides that have torn our national aspirations apart. We must change with the coming change of seasons. We must replace hatred with love, intolerance with openness, fear with boldness.

The next millennium begs for a new set of architects of a new society that shall be enshrined in morality, dignity for the African person and uncompromised liberty. These architects of an emancipated Africa and Zambia in particular, must be mobilised now. This will make up the new leadership that shall propel our generation into the next century.

One of the major goals of this generation of leaders should be to announce the year of the jubilee, when all third world countries would be forgiven of all their debt.

THE BIRTH OF THE COALITION

The key to a healed nation lies in the team chosen to handle the instruments of Government. The team must be patriotic, selfless and of strong character. What could destroy Zambia is not a lack of good laws, but a lack of good men and women to faithfully serve the people.

It is not enough to have a Christian President and Vice-President, but we will be more effective if we encouraged the people of morality who fear God to run for local Government and Parliament. Morality should start with the grass roots. The President will only be as effective as the people that surround him.

I believe that it takes a government that has conscience and morality to respect the voice of the Church. For the Church to be relevant, we must encourage people of conscience and morality to participate in politics. For two years now we have tried to reason with Government on issues we knew would bring suffering for the Zambian people in the long run. Issues of the constitution, dialogue, the tax placed on the Church for the first time in the history of the country, the blue book and license issues. We are all aware that these dreams have yet to be realised. We have therefore decided after more than ten months of con-

sultation that the best way to bring renewed hope to Zambia is by creating a new platform from which we can address national issues and practically participate in the formulation of policies that shall be Biblically anchored.

A third voice must now arise, whose pre-occupation shall not be confrontational politics, but that of preparing Zambia for the next century. I therefore with the authority of the Steering Committee, present to the Zambian people the NATIONAL CHRISTIAN COALITION, in short, NCC. This is not a political party, but a movement that shall spearhead a revolution of morality and prosperity for our land.

Some of the immediate objectives of the NCC shall be to:

1. *Sensitise, encourage and train people with morals anchored in the fear of God.*

2. *Formulate policies in all areas of the Zambian society based on Biblical values.*

3. *Participate in local and national elections with a view of infusing the system with God-fearing people.*

4. *Create a platform for wider participation of the citizens in the affairs of the nation.*

5. *Conduct a nation-wide civic education crusade.*

The Coalition shall target the moral majority of our population to participate in the affairs of the nation. We believe that, out there in the Districts and Provinces of our great nation lies untapped potential of God's generals that need to be encouraged and supported to play their God-ordained role of serving the nation.

THE CHALLENGE

Someone said "no one plans to fail, but many fail to plan." If Zambia fails in the next century it is because we have failed to adequately plan.

The social, spiritual and political atmosphere in our nation demands immediate attention from all Zambians. Until we achieve a certain measure of tolerance, love and forgiveness, our quest for prosperity will be totally unattainable.

For years now the Church and other civic organisations have tried to champion the cause of reconciliation in our nation, but with very little success if any at all. May I take this opportunity ladies and gentlemen to mention that my personal concerns about our peace process should not be viewed as being anti-government. I voted for this Government, and I have dear friends currently serving in Government. I have major problems with the attitude of the opposition for the most part, but usually address Government on most issues because they hold the scepter (key) of authority, and I have personally been involved in trying to reconcile the two sides and it is my firm belief that Government has more power to diffuse the tension in the nation than the other side. Esther in the Bible said to Mordecai, ***. . .all the King's servants, and the people of the King's provinces, do know, that whoever, whether man or woman, shall come into the King into the inner court, who is not called, there is one law of his to put him to death, except such to whom the King shall hold out the golden scepter, that he may live.***

This press conference has not been called to catalog either the failures or successes of our present government, but to find a common strategy to help put Zambia on top in the next century.

THE PLACE OF THE CHURCH

Whenever Zambia has a crucial football game, our foremost pre-occupation has never been the ball or stadium to be used, but the best players. Our best players will still stand a chance on the most rugged field. The same seriousness with which we choose our national soccer team should be used in the selection of political leaders.

Since the days of colonisation, the Church has been told not to get involved in national issues: politics. I overheard a government minister last week say, "We advise church leaders to desist from commenting on national issues, but that they should concentrate only on church issues." This view is what will destroy Africa if it is allowed to go uncorrected. The church becomes an irrelevant part of the society the moment it stops to infuse Government with morality. Morality is priority in most religions. Every individual and institution in Zambia should offer something to Government and the Church will offer the commodity it has — morality. Church's involvement in politics is not just a good idea, but a necessity.

The membership of the coalition will remain open to all Zambians. Those who aspire for office would have to satisfy the NCC code of ethics, which will be anchored in pro-life, pro-liberty and pro-family values.

Mobilisation of membership starts shortly after this press conference and will spread throughout the nation in the next few months. We shall conduct civic clinics in all the one hundred and fifty constituencies, and the educational seminars in the churches and through our on going partnership with credible NGOs whose objectives are similar to ours.

We shall continue to support and encourage Government to pursue politics that will stand the test of time. We are not an opposition, but a proposition of new ideas.

Zambians are aware that a number of us have tried our best to help bring reconciliation, and in the process have been misunderstood by both sides. The Bible says, ***My Spirit shall not continually strive with man. . . .*** *We should not subject the future of Zambia to unresolved personal issues. We need to turn around and plan an alternative strategy that will unite our people again.*

I sense a strong call on my life to be a part of a movement of healing. Healing of the social, spiritual and political landscape of our nation. I know how God speaks to me. I know His voice, and I have heard it loud and clear, "Mobilise, encourage and raise up an alternative force to steer this nation into the next millennium."

PROPHETIC CHALLENGE TO THE CHURCH

The founding of the National Christian Coalition comes at a very critical time in the life of the Church in our nation. Our cords of unity appear weak and disjointed, but it is through our weakness that strength will be perfected.

May I throw a challenge to my fellow clergy, and the body of Christ at large. I believe that the capacity to understand the times remains as a crucial aspect of our faith. Our victory, survival and success depend on this great truth.

While we may differ in the style of our preaching and doctrine, we should never compromise on our Judeo-Christian values.

If we don't stand together and deliberately prepare leadership from our ranks, the next century could be our darkest. We should not be overtaken by those whose interests are based on personal consumption.

The issue of the presidency does not even arise. Our present situation teaches us volumes on this subject. Three Christians in Government will not be sufficient to turn the boat around. We may not have as much resource as the western countries, but we have moral men and women who can take the challenge if encouraged. The western countries can afford to have bad leaders for a while, but most third world countries cannot, because we have limited resources that must be carefully distributed by a moral leadership to benefit all.

We need a fresh start for a new millennium. Third World debt does not make a lot of sense to many people, but when we link it to a lack of funding for health clinics, and schools then most people would agree to the realities of our plight.

HOW IT BEGAN

In the late 1970s and early 1980s, when richer nations were taken to lend money at good interest rates, the governments of many Third World countries took loans. The money was used to build roads, hospitals, government building, dams, and all too often, weapons.

For a few years everyone was happy. Then two things happened which sent the debt crisis spiraling out of control. Prices of many of the goods exported by third World countries such as cotton, coffee, rubber and tea dropped sharply. Interest rates soared around the world. Loans which had been reasonably easy to repay suddenly became huge burdens to governments now lacking foreign exchange. Repayments could not be met in full and the debt burdens began to grow.

IN THE 1990s

Today the situation has become worse. Many governments are forced to spend far more on debt repayments than on providing health care and education for their people. For example, Africa now spends four times more on interest on its loans than on health care.

Governments don't like to talk much about the issue either in the lending or borrowing countries — for both it has become an embarrassment. Ordinary people find the situation quite complicated to understand — debts have been sold to all kinds of banks and companies. But the simple truth is the Third World debt has become a kind of slavery, depriving millions of their rights to health care and education. There is need for the support of the on-going jubilee 2000, a debt free start for a billion people. Jubilee 2000 is asking for the beginning of the millennium to be a time when the backlog of the unpayable Third World debt is canceled.

Many economists and business people believe this is a business-like approach to solving an awkward situation. Caring people believe this is a moral solution to an impossible situation. Many Christians believe this to be prophetic and in line with God's purpose to celebrate the new millennium as a year of jubilee.

Another major goal of this new generation of political leaders should be to insist that politics are handled by people of the highest values, morality and integrity. The fair distribution of goods and services in any nation depends on the morality of its leadership.

A third goal should be to change the negative sting that surround politics and politicians. A new leaf has to be turned.

The people we lead in our churches are waiting for us to be relevant to the issues affecting our nation. Our silence speaks of our irrelevance and I see a great movement of irrelevant churches becoming relevant. Christians have questions on justice, participation and morality, and we must supply the answers, otherwise, we declare ourselves irrelevant.

A number of years ago Christians were discouraged from studying law, medicine, and being involved in business. We are still paying a high price for that high level of ignorance. The last frontier to be possessed by a people of morality is that of politics. For long we have discouraged our members from being involved in politics, this attitude is detrimental to the survival of the African continent. The question is no longer, should I be involved in politics? But rather, how and when should I get involved?

We sit like Esther in the palace of our ministries, and I hear the voice of Mordecai saying, ***Think not with yourself that thou shalt escape in the King's house, more than all the Jews. For if thou altogether holdest thy peace at this time, then shall deliverance arise from another place, but thou and thy father's house shall be destroyed; and who knowest whether thou art come to the kingdom for such a time as this?***

We sound the call for all those who have identified this season to climb on board and prepare our nation for the next millennium.

Those who are ready and available, we propose, you take off your high heels, and suits and let us take this message to every village of our country, that the seasons have changed and we need to raise the standard of our nation. With God on our side, strength and love in our hearts, victory is certain.

Thank you, and may God bless our great country.[19]

The formation of the NCC movement drew ample media attention:

Outspoken President of Victory Ministries International Pastor Nevers Mumba will launch a new political movement tomorrow, it was learned in Lusaka yesterday. Pastor Mumba, who of late in his sermons and press statements has carpeted African leaders (with) corruption and vote manipulation said the time has come for the church to offer alternative leadership.[20]

[19]NCC Formation Speech. Given by Dr. Nevers Mumba at a press conference held at the Pamodzi Hotel in Lusaka, 11:00 Hours, 04 September 1997.

[20]Moses Mbewe, "Nevers Eyes Plot One?" *The Daily Mail*, 03 September 1997.

Mixed reaction has greeted Dr. Nevers Mumba's entry into the political arena, a move that has also generated much interest in political circles as well as the church. . . . Zambia, as indeed many other African countries, is in dire need of men and women of integrity, imbued with a sense of purpose and direction; individuals willing to render selfless service. The public has become highly distrustful of politicians because the bulk seem obsessed with personal aggrandizement. Public service has become a source of enrichment for many.[21]

At a packed press conference at Pamodzi Hotel, Pastor Mumba. . said the NCC, despite making its intentions known to participate in local and national elections, was not a political party, 'but a movement that shall spearhead a revolution of morality and prosperity' for Zambia.[22]

Emmanuel Chilekwa had this to say in his 9 September 1997 civic education column entitled "Nevers' Move Makes Politicians Nervous":

This is where I personally appreciate Nevers Mumba's approach of having a morally upright leadership for the next millennium. . . . To those that never had the opportunity to listen to Nevers, the fibre of his message is around getting and then training a morally upright leadership for the challenges of the next millennium.

Our politicians have never been used to resigning on their own accord unless forced by a tribunal or the Court of Law. Or, perhaps, fired by the President. Why? Simple. Because their conscience is not in them. "It takes one with a conscience to understand conscience," Nevers said. "Some of our leaders are below par, in almost all respects. They have numerous faults, they have several wives and numerous concubines, they are rarely sober and lack self control."

Other editorials read:

Truth and boldness has been lacking on the part of our government. The nation awaits with awe when the Gabon Air disaster report will be made known to the nation (since 1993). . . . Unless our government learns to tell the hard truth, it will continue losing integrity in the eyes of the citizenry. We have had enough of poverty, enough of potholes, enough of witch-hunting, name it. We need a new breed, an

[21]Opinion, *The Zambia Post*, 05 September 1997.

[22]Moses Mbewe, *The Daily Mail*, 05 September 1997.

upright lot to manage our meagre resources. We welcome Dr. Mumba's new movement with open hands — it is good news. . . .[23]

> ***We have had enough of poverty, enough of potholes, enough of witch-hunting. . .***

Now Nevers Mumba is making a lot of people nervous. I am not exactly sure why, but I suspect it has to do with Frederick Chiluba's job. Not that the good pastor wants to go to Plot Number One, Independence Avenue, Lusaka. Well, not immediately anyway. On that score, a lot of prayer is being offered. Happily, I have not been made nervous as a result of the formation of the National Christian Coalition. I happen to agree with Pastor Mumba. . . in so far as the coalition intends to call the political establishment to account for their moral and ethical quality.[24]

A day or two after the public formation of the NCC, a top official of the MMD went on television in an unsuccessful effort to dismantle Mumba's speech. Every paragraph of the NCC speech was dissected and discredited. This lightning-quick reaction from the MMD's top brass showed they were indeed nervous of Nevers and his new NCC. The media's assessment was accurate: the MMD were allergic to public accountability.

The nation's leading monthly business magazine, *Profit*, put Dr. Mumba, donning a lilac suit, on the front cover of their October 1997 issue. *Profit* sent reporter Theo Bull to interview Nevers. The article, entitled "This Turbulent Priest," with accompanying colour photos by Francois d'Elbee, is my favourite article on Nevers. Bull had this to say about whether Mumba would be a fizzling firework or a rising star:

The MMD is running scared of Nevers Mumba. Any TV watcher or newspaper reader can see that at a glance. Do they have good reason to be? I suggest they do, for he has things going for him that any establishment is liable to be scared of.

He is a 'turbulent priest' in the tradition of Thomas à Becket, Martin Luther or Martin Luther King — or for that matter Trevor Huddleston or our own Colin Morris.

[23]Opinion, "A Timely Action," *Chronicle View*, 09 September 1997.
[24]Opinion, "NCC Right On," *Benchmark Editorial*, 09 September 1997.

He is not some easy-to-handle opponent from outside, but a rebel from deep within the new establishment.

Having already a considerable public following and no known skeletons in his cupboard, he could well become a powerful, even a passionate, spokesman for the Zambian masses. . . .

The NCC leaders see a great need both among the clergy of all denominations and among the general public, for increased public awareness, information and debate on a vast range of economic, social and political issues. They see a need, too, for voter mobilisation and voter registration, for a far closer working relationship with MPs and their constituents, for a better information flow to chiefs and headmen, for a freer and more democratic system of local government, and even for the beginning of democracy in schools. It is, for me, a truly impressive list of aspirations, and if only a few of them were achieved Zambia would be a better place to live in.

On moral issues I believe that a great many people across society would support Mumba's sober views. 'Life is one whole entity,' he says. 'If a man cannot handle his home life, and you put him into Government, you cannot expect him to perform well with those larger responsibilities. If people cannot control themselves in their private life, how will they do so when they have taxpayers' money and cars and fuel at their disposal? They are very likely to start abusing their government position.'

Mumba sees the need 'for a good screening system.' 'We are not looking for angels or perfect people but people of conscience to hold public office.'

...Nevers Mumba, it seemed to me, saw the MMD as too narrowly political and too politically narrow. 'They can't run the country alone. For them, if you don't belong, you're a black sheep. They have to make people feel important and feel involved....Now, instead of a Republican President, it's a party President ruling this nation....There's a need for a national spirit that is missing.'

In short, I found in Nevers Mumba a passionate concern, which I believe to be genuine, a clear brain and serious application to public issues. He is an encouraging new phenomenon in the tired world of Zambian politics.[25]

After winning the 1991 election, Frederick Chiluba had selected Brigadier-General Godfrey Miyanda to be his Vice-President. The tall and handsome Miyanda is considered by many to possess Zambia's sharpest military mind. General Miyanda is also a spirit-filled Christian. It was my privilege to be on stage with General

[25]Theo Bull, "This Turbulent Priest," *Profit*, October 1997, 29–32.

Miyanda and his wife at the 1995 VM International Conference and watch the two of them worship freely. Once MMD won the October 1996 election, the Zambian papers looked ahead to the fall of 2001 for Zambia's third president and it surprised Nevers to see his name make the list as a "dark horse" while the front runner was Vice-President Miyanda. A year later Chiluba demoted Miyanda to Minister of Education. The move shocked everyone, including the Vice President. Rumblings came out of MMD headquarters that Chiluba was contemplating changing his own constitutional ammendment to let his name stand in the 2001 election. Nobody in MMD was going to get in his way.

This type of insecurity, tyranny and confusion unfortunately but accurately describes the MMD's ten-year administration. Kenneth Kaunda, Nevers Mumba, Godfrey Miyanda and Dean Mung'omba were considered by the papers in 1996 to be among the front runners for the 2001 presidency. Subsequently, all four men have had questionable attacks on their character or worse, on their lives. Kaunda has resigned from politics, Miyanda has technically dropped from the presidential race. Of those four men, only two are still in the race: ZAP's[26] Dean Mung'omba and NCC's Nevers Mumba. Since the 1996 newspaper article, two new men have let their name stand for president. Ben Mwila, the ousted MMD defense minister and treasurer, leads his Republican Party, and the former Central African Director of Anglo-American, Anderson Mazoka, will run on the United Party for National Development (UPND) ticket.

It would have been arduous in the early 1990s for President Chiluba to locate a bigger supporter in North America than me. Throughout the 1980s, Nevers and I strategised how Zambia could be reached with the gospel. What better way to foster a nationwide openness to Christianity than to have a Christian President? I will always remember the honour of having lunch at State House and of watching the video of the President weeping at the football funeral. It appears to me, a Canadian who loves Zambian people, that Frederick Chiluba sincerely wanted to make Zambia a Christian nation. However, by publicly renouncing political corruption in 1991, he only initiated the battle. To win this war the President needed to ceaselessly annihilate every root of corruption in public office. This should have included the prompt dismissal of several of his avaricious officials who shamelessly used their position for per-

[26]In an effort to prevent vote-splitting in the 2001 election, Mung'omba's ZDC party had amalgamated with a few other parties to form the new Zambia Alliance for Progress Party, or ZAP.

sonal gain rather than public service. This is what FTJ failed to do. He surrounded himself with unethical political advisers who sadly led him astray. Instead of changing the system, the system changed him.

9

NATIONAL CITIZENS' COALITION

Zambia has always strived to be a nation of freedom. The red stripe on their national flag represents the human blood spilled in the fight for freedom. The eagle on Zambia's flag and coat of arms symbolises freedom. The most famous statue in Zambia is the Freedom Statue in downtown Lusaka that poignantly depicts freedom from colonial oppression while the words "free" and "freedom" appear seven times in Zambia's national anthem. Despite recent political setbacks, freedom remains an important issue to Zambians.

Christianity produces personal freedom, therefore the gospel should be well received in Zambia and is, as evidenced by the minimal resistance to the Christian declaration made by President Chiluba in 1991. But ten years later, Zambians are disillusioned and disappointed because their nation is now in noticeably worse shape than before it became a "Christian" nation.

> *The revelation by the United Nations agency's Common Country Assessment (CCA) report that over 80% of Zambians cannot afford to meet the basic nutritional requirements as a result of a general drop in real incomes in the 1990s is frightening....*
>
> *The report says there has been a growing trend of food insecurity in Zambia both at a national and household level in the 1990s. Clearly, and despite all the claimed achievements in monetary policies, all is not well in Zambia, especially in the social sector....*
>
> *Even if our country has been declared a Christian nation there is no spirit of sharing what the nation has. We have gross inequalities, with some having more than they need and dying of heart attacks and cholesterol, while others starve to death.*
>
> *Here we don't share — as if our country doesn't belong to all of us, and its riches to all of us, too. Here, more than 80% of our citizens*

feel they don't count; they are not a part of society; they don't feel they have a national dignity and a homeland.

We are talking about the things that, in our opinion, constitute true humanitarianism, the policy of promoting the dignity of human beings and their well-being. Inequality causes terrible suffering.

In the light of our experiences over the last nine years, there is no need for the government to resist the neoliberal policies it is pursuing — the policies that have ruined the lives of most of our people, including most of our businessmen, to the benefit of transnational corporations and their local agents. We cannot talk of democracy and human rights in a country pursuing policies that only benefit a small, powerful and rich minority at the expense of over 80% of the citizens who wallow in extreme poverty. This is really a strange democracy where the great majority counts for nothing.[27]

Since being summoned to the State House that edgy September morning in 1990, Pastor Mumba has served as a spiritual advisor to both presidents, but he did not have his eye on the presidency. He simply burned with the passion that "Zambia Shall Be Saved!" History needs to remember that Mumba's counsel to, and prayer with, President Kaunda that morning in 1990 helped to stave off bloodshed in Zambia.

History also cannot ignore the fact that after only three weeks in office, it was President Chiluba who initiated contact with Nevers. Political pundits have accused Nevers of using his contacts with the first two Zambian presidents to bolster his chances of becoming the third president. That simply was not the case.

It is imperative for one to understand the context in which Nevers created the National Christian Coalition. The MMD government chose not to practice what they preached. Chiluba's brand of confused Christianity is the antithesis of what Pastor Mumba envisioned for his beloved nation when he returned home in 1984. Integrity must be paramount in a Christian government, but it became almost nonexistent. The gospel brings clarity not confusion, but as the second term began for the MMD, Dr. Mumba felt compelled to address the mess. Few church leaders supported the outspoken Mumba because they feared the backlash. Nevers simply could not remain silent any longer about the blatant hypocrisy of the Christian government.

[27]Editorial, "Our Strange Democracy," *The Post of Zambia*, 14 December 2000.

The government repeatedly attempted to depict Nevers as backsliding from the ministry to enter politics, but the truth is Nevers presently serves as both the President of Victory Ministries and the Chairman of the National Citizens' Coalition.

As Nevers' closest friend, I could see this battle waging in his astute mind. Can God ask a pastor to also be a politician? Joseph, Esther and Daniel are but three examples from the Bible of people used by God in the political arena of their day. God therefore does not appear to have a problem combining faith with politics. But some people do.

To let Nevers know that I saw his struggle, I brought him some political science textbooks during one of my visits to Zambia. We stayed up late one night in his Kitwe home as he explained his situation. I was honored that he confided such guarded information with me.

Nevers sees eye-to-eye with his close friends that include Ghana's Mensa Otabil, South Africa's Kenneth Meshoe and me. Notwithstanding, since the early 1980s Nevers has looked up to Reinhard Bonnke, Freda and Dennis Lindsay and Carlton Pearson. Nevers' plan was to bounce his idea off Bonnke, the Lindsays, me, and if he could ever meet with him, Carlton. Nevers started with me. After listening at length, I encouraged him to run. I told him that I could see it coming and that is why I brought the textbooks. My only advice to Nevers that night was to be as energetic in politics as he had been in preaching. "If you're going to run, you must run to win," were my exact words.

Nevers wrote Reinhard. It seemed to me that Bonnke's approval meant the most to Nevers since they were both African crusade evangelists. Subsequently Nevers found it dejecting when the Apostle to Africa took two years to answer. Pastor Bonnke never forgot about Nevers' letter. However, he took his time prayerfully contemplating the evangelistic ramifications of this possible ministry shift. Bonnke's tardy decision came in an e-mail; he encouraged Nevers to run for State House in 2001. Bonnke also agreed to write an endorsement for this book.

While waiting for Reinhard's reply, Nevers met with the venerable Mom Lindsay and her son Dennis in Dallas. Dennis was now the President and CEO of CFN. Before commenting himself on the proposal, Dennis requested and received permission from Nevers to run the idea by their advisory team at CFN. While some on the

CFN Council quoted Billy Graham's famous response that it is a demotion for a preacher to become President, another man, Dr. Eric Belcher, who had instructed Nevers, Florence, Heidi and me back in 1984, displayed great insight when he encouraged the CFN team not to force American thinking onto African politics. After more discussion, Dennis, his octogenarian mother and their advisory team gave Nevers the green light.

In the spring of 1999, Dr. Mumba and Bishop Carlton Pearson spent an hour together in Carlton's office, praying and talking over the idea. Carlton was highly supportive and made a couple of calls to prominent black leaders in the USA who could possibly assist Nevers financially.

In retrospect, it would appear that by creating the NCC, Nevers hoped to oppose the unchecked injustice in the existing government while keeping VM's national influence strong and vibrant. When the efforts of the NCC were either ridiculed or castigated by the MMD, Nevers went on the offensive. Nine months after formulating the National Christian Coalition, his executive voted unanimously to change their name to National Citizens' Coalition and to change their manifesto to become a political party. Their ambitious goal: lead Zambia with an ethical government in the new century. The line was drawn in the sand, and Nevers stepped over the line. There was no turning back. He felt compelled to assist his beloved Zambia live up to its potential as a Christian nation. When questioned about his political intentions, Nevers answered, "I am here to put Christianity into action." He would let his name stand for President in 2001.

> *On 4th September 1997, we launched the National Christian Coalition with the main objective of identifying and mobilising leaders of morality to participate in the national governance issues. The past ten months have produced a tremendous season of growth for us, but it has also been an uphill battle with the MMD government using the machinery of its media to discredit our participation on a non-partisan basis. We thought that Zambia was a democracy where political parties and movements were allowed not only to be registered, but also to function. We have since discovered that the MMD wants to be the only political player. They have . . . imprisoned, changed the constitution . . . and broken all electoral rules by using government resources and vehicles to campaign.*

Since we cannot reason with or advise our government on anything from the outside as we had intended, the National Council of the NCC yesterday, 19th June 1998, decided to register a new political party in the name of National Citizens' Coalition. The new name is meant to portray our goal of becoming a mass party, and not restricted to one group of the population. Our goal is to be the strongest party in the land, run for elections and form the next government.

Zambia deserves better and Zambia shall get better.

I now wish to address myself to my fellow Christians and to those who have risen to criticise my personal involvement in national issues. I find no better way to please God than to do what He would do if He were here today, touching people at their point of need. I will never stop preaching the Gospel of Christ. It is not a garment that one puts on and takes off at another time. This is my life; to be in the will of God. I feel more fulfilled to both preach and practically help my nation.

History is full of Christians who have influenced and changed their nations and generation: Reverend Martin Luther King Jr. had a dream and dared to stand up to an unjust government, Reverend Jesse Jackson brought the hope for a better future to African-Americans while Reverend Pat Robertson of CBN ran for the US presidency in 1988.

I have come with a clear message today for my fellow citizens. It is time to say NO to corruption,
NO to violence,
NO to vengeance,
NO to injustice,
NO to lies.

Come now and join hands with us in NCC to address these failures.

Zambians are crying for agricultural inputs and credits — we hear you.

Zambians are crying for better and affordable education — we hear you.

Zambians are crying for jobs — we hear you.

There is a cry for justice — we hear you.

There is a cry for better and affordable health services — we hear you.

There is a cry to recognise womens' rights — we hear you.

There is a cry for development — we hear you.

> *Our party shall work to transform Zambia as rapidly as possible into a united, multi-racial, multi-ethnic, non-sexist democracy.*
>
> *Our party shall work for one Zambia, one people with a shared destiny for all the people of Zambia.*
>
> *We are poised for a new chapter in the history of our nation. You can make a difference. Join the second wind of change. I therefore make a firm commitment to all NCC members nation-wide, and the people of Zambia that I will fight with determination until Zambia sees a new day of hope. We shall never retreat. The battle is on and Zambia shall be saved.*[28]

This significant shift in ministry focus carried a heavy price tag for Nevers and his dedicated VM team as the MMD offensive against them only intensified. Since Pastor Mumba had left the holy perch of preaching and "backslid" into the quagmire of ignoble politics, the ruling party stated he no longer qualified for the diplomatic passport. When it came time for Dr. Mumba to renew his passport, his diplomatic status was revoked. Victory Ministries' television contract with ZNBC was not renewed, forcing *Zambia Shall Be Saved* temporarily off the air. When VM approached ZNBC about purchasing air time, the station refused, stating the MMD had given them clear orders to keep the face of Nevers Mumba off TV. Next, the Christian government placed tax assessments on the Victory Bible Church in Kitwe. The MMD felt that since Dr. Mumba had become a politician, his ministry should be taxed, retroactive four years. The fact that Nevers was still the Senior Pastor of the Victory Bible Church did not seem to matter. The government was sending Zambia's top religious leader a far-from-subtle message: Politics is about power and you will not get into power without a dirty fight.

Special Branch officers, Zambia's equivalent of the CIA, attended NCC meetings and Victory services in stealth and then reported back to State House. People who sided with Dr. Mumba were harassed and NCC donors found their bank accounts mysteriously frozen, making it impossible for any Zambian of means to donate to the new party. Nevers and Florence realised that their home phone was not secure when excerpts of private phone conversations were later repeated by government officials. Their e-mail was traced, making it difficult for them to communicate confidentially with anyone. Even postal letters were subject to scrutiny.

[28]Speech given by NCC Chairman, Dr. Nevers Mumba, at the NCC rally in Kabwe, 20 June 1998.

Nevers' every move was followed closely, not only in Zambia. Political fair play is an African oxymoron.

> ***Political fair play is an African oxymoron.***

The author witnessed this sneaky conduct first-hand. Due to the intensifying conflict with government, Nevers temporarily moved the Victory Ministry's headquarters and national conference to Windhoek, Namibia. However, running from the MMD is what the ruling government hoped Victory Ministries would do. Thus, Pastors Mumba and Nsofu decided to host their 1999 International Conference back in Lusaka. Along with Kenneth Meshoe, and a few other pastors from southern Africa, I was listed as one of the invited speakers that August. The Mulungushi Centre, undergoing major renovations in preparations for a fall symposium on AIDS in Africa, was not available. This left the Intercontinental Hotel (Intercon) Ballroom. As a guest of Victory, I had always stayed at the Pamodzi Hotel and was actually looking forward to the change of venue. Furthermore, the government-influenced "Intercon" is located a stone's throw from the major international embassies and I had hoped to visit Canada's High Commission while in Lusaka. Upon clearing customs at the airport I was surprised to discover that I would be returning to the five-star Pamodzi Hotel and that the Mulungushi Centre was once again the venue for the conference. Though usually curious and full of questions, I was too jet-lagged to care and gladly went to sleep at the privately-run Pamodzi. Nevers arrived in Lusaka two days later and explained the abrupt changes to me. There was reason to speculate the management of the Intercontinental Hotel had been instructed by the MMD to host Victory's conference and then disallow the event only three days before it was to start. The idea was that under such short notice VM would have no place to hold their conference, humiliating themselves in front of their delegates and international guests. However, the MMD underestimated the tenacity of Pastors Mumba and Nsofu and Victory's veteran ministry team. VM promptly and painlessly moved the hotel reservations of their guests over to the Pamodzi. But now came the hard part — booking a large hall with three days notice. Nevers went personally to the key managers at the Mulungushi and secured their approval. Most of the renovations in the auditorium were complete so services could be held there while the construction crews worked elsewhere in the Centre.

It had been four years since I had been at the Mulungushi. In 1995, the Centre was packed daily with 3,000–5,000 delegates. The African music and singing was heavenly. Both President Chiluba and Vice-President Miyanda attended evening meetings. But now it was 1999. 'My how things changed in four years,' I thought to myself. The conference delegates had no way of knowing the venue change, justifying the poor attendance of that opening night. Instead of jubilant singing of thousands resounding off the walls, I was ushered into a renovated auditorium where a meager 100 believers were singing their hearts out to God in worship. The auditorium appeared cavernous this time. Luxurious new purple chairs had replaced the tired yellow ones in the main floor VIP section. But like the comfort of seeing a good friend in a strange place, the well-travelled, eight-year-old VM sound system was there to reassure me that although plenty had changed, plenty had stayed the same.

If the recent dirty tricks bothered Nevers, he didn't show on the opening night. He preached as well as I had ever heard him. Word slowly got around the city that the conference had moved and a respectable crowd had gathered by week's end.

When Nevers let his name stand for the 2001 presidency, both he and Florence realised that they could not effectively shepherd their wonderful congregation and run for State House. They pined over this decision but recognised that by remaining the Senior Pastors they would make their church more vulnerable to the vindictive MMD attacks. The Victory Bible Church had stood with the Mumbas all of these years, so releasing it was painful. The Mumbas resigned as the Senior Pastors on Easter Sunday, 1998, and turned the church over to their business-like associate Lubuto Nsofu. Throughout the Mumba's eleven year pastoral tenure the church had outgrown several different rented auditoriums throughout Kitwe. Eventually, the church received land from the government to build their own sanctuary and its construction is one of the major goals of Pastor Nsofu.

During this period, some of Nevers' ministry-friends in Zambia and in the West chose to disassociate themselves with the turbulent priest. His political motives were misunderstood both in Zambia and in North America, causing outside and inside financial assistance for VM and the Mumbas to dry up. It seemed to me that some of these people liked Nevers only as a preacher and not a politician. The Mumbas tried to sell their home on Jambo Drive, but were unsuccessful, due to the huge economic downturn in the Copperbelt. The government was in the process of privatising the copper mines, but the resulting debacle almost capsized the Zambian economy.

The decision to enter politics was taxing on Florence, too. Back at CFNI, she and Nevers had committed their lives to the Lord for efficacious gospel ministry, but now they were stepping away from the pastorate and going into politics. Their identity within Zambia's Christian community was secure. Their political identity in the nation was insecure.

A prominent politician secretly warned Nevers that the latter's name was on top of a government assassination list the former had seen accidentally. The date had been set for 23 December 1998. Pastor Mumba was advised to get his family away from their Kitwe home and not to drive the highways at night. Disguised men, brandishing AK-47s, climbed the walls of the Shalom Christian School campus that very night. They entered the building in stealth only to find it empty. The assailants went next to the resident caretaker's home, rudely woke him up and demanded that he tell them where Nevers Mumba was. The janitor answered honestly that he did not know where any of the Mumbas were. They tied him up and took another look around the school, but the custodian managed to wriggle free and immediately began shouting for help. Alarmed, the assassins fled, their mission a failure. After this life and death situation, God's promise of protection from Deuteronomy 28:7 became extra real to the Mumba family: **The LORD shall cause thine enemies that rise up against thee to be smitten before thy face: they shall come out against thee one way, and flee before thee seven ways.**

Even though the school custodian could positively identify one of the attackers, the local police took no action. This lack of justice upset the people of Kitwe. Security was tightened around the Mumba home. The NCC provided the Mumbas with a driver and bodyguards. To protect Nevers and his family from being poisoned NCC advisers instructed the Mumbas to only drink beverages from sealed bottles or to have an NCC bodyguard accompany anyone who was pouring a beverage for any member of the family.

Dr. Kaunda's closest and youngest son, Wezi, was not as fortunate. He was murdered outside his home in Lusaka on 04 November 1999. BBC World News reported it on television while in

Zambia, *The Observer* filed this report:

> *Wezi and his wife, Didre, were driving home to a suburb of Lusaka in his Toyota Landcruiser when they were approached by a group of armed men. According to Didre, Kaunda told the gang, "I am Major Wezi Kaunda. Please take my car, take whatever you want. I am not resisting. Spare my life and my wife. Just take the car." The gang replied, "We know who you are. Do you think we don't know? Shoot him." The men ordered Kaunda out of the car and shot him in the stomach, back and shoulder. He was rushed to hospital, where he died a few hours later. The car was found abandoned, but nothing had been taken.*[29]

Wezi was 47.

Dr. Kaunda asked Pastor Mumba, a long-time friend of Wezi's, to speak at the funeral and later at the memorial service. After Nevers finished speaking, Dr. Kaunda asked the people of Zambia, specifically the young men of his UNIP, to peacefully protest this wrongful death, for rumours had circulated Lusaka that UNIP-initiated riots would break out after the memorial service. Losing his son was too much for Kaunda; he officially resigned from politics four months later at age 75.

While dignitaries and government officials flew in from several countries to attend the memorial service, President Chiluba was conspicuous by his absence and his silence. No top minister in the MMD government attended either service nor offered any public condolences to the grieving Kaunda family. This conduct lent credence to the growing theory that Wezi's death was not a murder but a political assassination, for Wezi was being considered to replace his father as leader of UNIP.

Three senior detectives from Scotland Yard were brought in by the MMD to investigate the death of Major Wezi Kaunda. Their findings have yet to be published.

Nevers and KK had already been dialoguing before Wezi's tragic death. The author was present at one such meeting. The date was Thursday, 12 August and the 1999 VM International Conference was winding down. Nevers had planned to escort me that day to the airport for my afternoon British Airways flight to London. That morning, KK called Nevers and asked if they could meet while

[29]Tony Thompson, *The Observer*, 14 November 1999.

Nevers was still in Lusaka. Nevers picked me up early and told me that we were going to Dr. Kaunda's Kabulonga home for a visit. It would have been much easier for Nevers to just take me to the airport first and then meet with KK, but Nevers invited me, I felt, as a way of repaying the kindness I had shown him over the years. It was an exhilarating experience to meet Kenneth Kaunda in person. Nevers' aide took a picture of Kaunda, Nevers and me. "The white guy" looks uptight in the photo because he felt completely underdressed for such an occasion. Not only am I the only one not in a suit, I am wearing sandals without socks. Nonetheless, meeting KK was an honour. Nevers' driver then took me to the airport while Mumba and Kaunda met.

The two men wondered if a political alliance could be formed. UNIP is the nation's oldest and best-organised party, but they have no dominant leader to replace Kaunda. Nevers is a strong leader with a young, small party. Blending the two would produce an attractive product. I encouraged Nevers to seriously consider this option. UNIP youth leaders were for the arrangement too:

> *The Copperbelt UNIP youths are demanding a merger between UNIP and the National Citizens' Coalition (NCC) in their stepped up pressure for an outsider to lead the former ruling party.*
>
> *The youths, after a meeting held in Ndola yesterday, resolved to increase pressure on former president Kenneth Kaunda to accept their proposal to field NCC leader Nevers Mumba to stand as party president.*
>
> *The latest move was confirmed by the pressure group's leader Peter Mubili, who is UNIP Mufilira district youth chairman. "We want UNIP to merge with NCC and the name should change to United National Integrated Party (UNIP). We all want a leader of great credibility and a God-fearing man. Dr. Mumba is the best choice for this. We want to harmonise the camps which have been created."*
>
> *Meanwhile, the NCC has regretted the retirement of Dr. Kaunda... NCC national vice-chairperson Eva Sanderson, speaking of Kaunda, said, "His contribution to the region and the world at large cannot be ignored. We hope he will continue being available to us."*[30]

Some of these UNIP youth went so far as to proclaim a hunger strike until Dr. Mumba was elected their leader.

The dawning of the year 2001 has brought with it the increased

[30]Times Reporter, "Let Mumba Lead UNIP," *Times of Zambia*, 30 March 2000.

probability of a merger between Pastor Mumba and UNIP. Nevers has moved cautiously because this type of amalgamation makes him anxious. The NCC had previously encouraged him to attempt a merger with ZAP. Other political parties had banded together under ZAP banner with the recently divorced Dean Mung'omba at the helm. The NCC executive initially saw only the benefits of teaming up with ZAP. They didn't see the drawbacks; people in ZAP were not as firmly committed to the moral principles of the NCC. Eight months after they started conversing together, Nevers and his NCC team realised they could not work within the ZAP framework. This detour cost Nevers precious campaign time so he was hesitant about making another possible wrong turn with UNIP.

The NCC decided to publicise their ten-point plan. If other parties wanted to work with NCC, they would have to accept these points as non-optional:

1. Governance. Good governance is based on truth, tolerance, love and fair play. We propose a total separation of powers where the Executive, Judiciary and Legislative arms of government are independent. Upon constitutional amendment, members of parliament will not be expected to be cabinet ministers and visa versa. Cabinet ministers will be drawn from a wider sector of society regardless of their political party. Judges will be appointed by an independent judicial commission and not the Executive.

2. Opportunity. Citizens will find work in a growing, full employment economy. All workers will have the legal right to form unions of their choice and to bargain collectively for wages and conditions of employment. The NCC will ensure a society where our parents and the disabled can lead lives of dignity. We commit to unshakeable pension schemes.

3. Order. The NCC will endorse a zero tolerance for crime through strong and motivated defence and security wings. Stiff penalties await offenders.

4. Democracy. The NCC government will aggressively move to legally end all forms of public and private discrimination based upon race, sex, age, colour, creed, national origin, religion, economic status or political persuasion. We promote a strong, civil society based on responsibility and basic human rights.

5. Health. All Zambians are to have access to quality medical care on demand. We promote a clean environment for every citizen and primary health care through community participation.

6. Education. Education will be offered to all citizens as a basic human right. Education is fundamental to all sustainable human development. ALL Zambian children will be entitled to education up to secondary level. Tertiary education will be funded on the basis of repayable loans and a more skills-oriented curriculum will be offered to those who do not make it to higher institutions of learning.

7. Agriculture. NCC will maximise the use of arable land to attain food security for the first time in our nation's history. A nation that can not feed itself can not claim sovereignty. Government will assume a primary role in the distribution of farming inputs and irrigation. We will market and store produce through well-organised cooperatives in conjunction with traditional authorities. Rural development programmes will be intensified and credit facilities made available.

8. Local Government. Under the NCC there will be a devolution of powers, encouraging regional self-determination guided by central government and pooled at a national level to tackle common problems. The constituency will become the basic unit for development, determining its own priority areas. Traditional rulers will be incorporated and recognised as the oldest institution of authority.

9. Technology. Zambia desperately needs modern infrastructure in mining, agriculture, tourism, communication and energy to compete favourably in the global economy. Training of manpower and minimising our "brain drain" in this sector will be our priority. Incentives to stimulate and encourage the local manufacturing industry will be determined in consultation with stakeholders.

10. Household. NCC will encourage a society that strengthens families and protects children. We will create a national database through information technology (IT) to account for every citizen within the borders of Zambia. This will become the basis for national economic planning and widening of the tax base, which will be based clearly on the ability to pay. Social safety nets, in conjunction with the church and civic organisations, will be set up to alleviate and eradicate the poverty that dominates over 70% of Zambia's population.

One thing remained constant during all this upheaval — Nevers' passion:

The Chairman, Kitwe Press Club, executive members of the club, distinguished guests, ladies and gentlemen, thank you for the honour of inviting me to address you on NCC's vision for the next millennium.

The decision has been made. There is no looking back. With God on our side and the people of Zambia thrilled at the prospect of change, we feel confident that victory is certain.

NCC has come at a time of great distress for the Zambians, a time of uncertainty and a time of hopelessness. It has in principle restored hope for a better tomorrow. The Bible says ***weeping may endure for a night, but joy comes in the morning.*** *God has finally heard the cry of His people. Our tomorrow does not need to be like today. This century does not need to follow us into the next. We can make a break. A break from perpetual poverty, hatred, fear and confusion. A new day awaits all of us that are ready to run with the NCC.*

OUR VALUES

Zambia needs a new set of values upon which to base our recovery programme. Values that are consistent, values that are enshrined in the truth of God's word. NCC insists that there is no moral government in the absence of a moral leadership. We are also aware that there is no morality unless it is derived from God's moral laws. My humble submission, therefore, is that morality only exists within the framework of religion. The values of NCC will be based on respect for God-given liberties to man regardless of sex, tribe or political persuasion.

May I take this opportunity, Mr. Chairman, to address all the NCC members country-wide that we shall not engage ourselves in unnecessary political squabbles as this type of politics should be left for parties who have spare time.

NCC has no spare time to sling mud at anyone. Our only concern will be for Zambia to get better. I shall entertain no insults from NCC leaders for those in the ruling Party or any other Party. No derogatory terminology should be used in our rallies. Now that we are a Party, we must work on our programme of how we shall run government.

MMD members are not our enemies; they are our contemporaries. NCC values all the good things that UNIP and MMD have done for our country. If you supported us to form government we shall take all that is good from the past and mesh it with all our aspirations for the future. But we shall also be realistic and courageous to correct the wrongs that have beset our country.

Insulting a leader does not improve his performance. That is why you have not heard me use bad language against individuals in government. We should, however, speak against bad government policy and those leaders whose personal conduct is detrimental to the well-being of the nation. I will stick to issues and I ask all our leaders to do the same. Let other politicians insult but let NCC consult. Let other politicians lie, but let NCC learn from others. As they kill, let us care. Our goal is to have a new and free nation in the next century, where Zambians can eat food of their choice, where our children can go to schools of their choice, where Zambians can associate with any grouping of their choice without intimidation.

NCC strongly stands against:
1) Violence
2) Corruption
3) Vengeance
4) Injustice
5) Lies
These five evils will always remain the major enemies for the NCC.

ISSUES OF CONCERN

May I start by acknowledging the efforts made by the MMD government, especially in creating a free market economy. This was a courageous decision. I commend President Chiluba for boldly declaring Zambia a Christian nation. I have gone through the MMD manifesto and it is an excellent document. My question is: How come the government has failed to realise its ideals? One of my quick responses is that the team that was entrusted with the challenge had no moral power to carry out the programme. To win a football match, you need more than a good ball and stadium, you also need a good team. Some newspaper column last week said, 'NCC has not offered anything new....' Yes, it has. We are offering a leadership of morality and integrity.

1. ELECTORAL PROCESS

Now that NCC is a political party, it has to help in ensuring fairness in the electoral process. Government has decided to play hardball with the issue of dialogue on the constitution and the electoral process. I believe it is time the opposition also decided to play hardball. The Opposition should hold together for the first time and demand that the ruling Party allow for free and fair elections. Government has changed nothing in the electoral process since the controversial 1996 election. Now we seem to be heading for another controversial local government election. We should not, and must not, ignore dialogue before any election is held. May I warn government that the opposition is more united now than during the pre-1996 elections. Government will soon expose itself to further condemnation from the donor community if they dare conduct local government elections in the absence of dialogue. I appeal to all opposition parties not to break rank in this regard. We therefore demand dialogue, rules and regulations before any election.

2. EDUCATION

It is the belief of the NCC that our survival as a nation in the next century depends on educating our population.

The Bible says, ***You reap what you sow.*** *The Zambian government is trying to develop Zambia's economy without developing those who shall man the economy in the next century.*

We only have one university with two campuses. If we don't take care of our highest source of human resource for the future, who will do it for us? This is selfish for those of us that benefitted from government-assisted education. The government White Paper must be revisited and made relevant to the demands and challenges of a new century. The money spent on the Commission of Enquiry could afford many students an opportunity to earn a degree in the interest of the nation. Zambia has no choice on the issue of aggressive education for all Zambians. This shall be our life-line in the next century. Education is the basis for all development in health, agriculture, industry, management and, above all, confidence, which will be a necessary tool in the next century. Who shall operate the Internet? Who shall assemble and fly the jets of the future? Who shall mechanise and computerise new agricultural options? It is time to pull our resources together and make an investment with the future. We may not live long enough to see the fruit of our investment, but our children will.

OUR WAY FORWARD

My goal is to initiate a nation-wide campaign to offer information to my fellow Zambians that we should set higher standards for ourselves as a nation. We should not accept the present poverty or any leader who has failed to deliver goods. We deserve better and we shall get better. NCC is also concerned about MMD's insensitivity to tribal balancing. Zambia does not comprise of the Bemba kingdom alone. Thus, we must fight for a united nation. It is because of this trend that NCC has decided to put together a representative government when it takes office. Deserving Zambians who do not belong to NCC will also be considered for Cabinet.

I now would like to make an open call to all Zambians who feel things should change to come out in the open and fight this fight of faith. NCC invites all, and I mean all, fellow citizens who have Zambia's interests at heart to come join hands with us to do what is right for our country. I thank you all and may the Lord bless our great nation.[31]

Zambians were unsure of what was happening to Pastor Mumba. Was he still a pastor? How come he and Chiluba were no longer friends? Can Nevers win the presidency with the NCC or must he team up with UNIP? One thing was certain, this crucible of pressure was forging Nevers into a stronger man. Even Carlton Pearson noticed that Nevers was becoming more presidential. I noticed that Nevers could now comfortably discuss both economics and Ephesians.

He was also developing the highly refined skill of sermonising his speeches:

I believe in Zambia. I also believe in the Zambian people. We have what it takes to move our country out of this valley of the shadow of death. History encourages us with nations that had sunk and yet through a unified resolve, ended up on top. America in the early 1930s underwent an economic depression. Nobody could have imagined then that one day America would be the super power it is today.

The nation of Israel was in bondage for centuries, yet was mirac-

[31]Speech by Nevers Mumba to the Kitwe Press Club, 25 June 1998.

ulously born in May 1948, exactly 50 years ago.

South Africa, shackled by the chains of Apartheid, stood up against it and broke the chains of bondage.

There is hope for Zambia. Hope for us to transform ourselves into a prosperous nation.

Speaking at the University of Zambia School of Medicine in Lusaka on 2 September 1998, Dr. Mumba had this to say:

Ladies and gentlemen, tonight I have the privilege of addressing the cream of our intellectual community. If you can't make things happen in this country, no one else will. You are highly enlightened and civilised. If I can manage to inspire you to greatness, I will forever be thankful to God. My greatest disappointment would be to hear you say, "It's not that bad." Zambia can be better and it shall be better. You can sow a seed into the future by your resolve tonight.

Let me now make the unfortunate announcement: Zambia is in a crisis. A crisis politically, socially and economically. Hopelessness has settled in and a spirit of resignation fills the atmosphere in Zambia. The nation has become so dispirited. All that remains is a fragmented society. As you study in the Higher Institute of Learning, jobs are being exported to other countries. Hospitals have become haunted houses, no longer called health centres but dying centres. We have thousands of University and College graduates roaming the streets. Is there anything we can do to reverse this trend? I believe the solution to Zambia's crisis is within us.

All of the political pressure in Zambia did help the cause of African evangelism. During the period that VM had their international conference and ministry headquarters in Windhoek, Namibia, doors to the gospel opened in that former German colony. The International Conference, held at the prestigious Safari Court Hotel, was broadcast live on television across the nation. The VM crusades helped break the colour barrier and opened the door for the *Zambia Shall Be Saved* television program to be aired across Namibia. The new title? *Namibia Shall Be Saved.* The preaching segments for the show came from Pastor Mumba's ministry in Zambia. When preaching in Zambia, Pastor Mumba is prone to speaking a little in Bemba, which is foreign to Namibians. Despite this distraction, the show was hugely popular in Namibia.

This gave Nevers the courage to attempt something in August 1998 that, by African standards, was incredible. Pastor Mumba would preach from Windhoek's Safari Court Hotel and broadcast it live, via satellite, back to Zambia. Ghanian Pastor Mensa Otabil would open the live broadcast by welcoming the viewers and introducing Nevers. The $15,000 bill, the majority of which came from the Namibian Broadcast Corporation, was secondary to the massive technological concerns. But typical of Nevers, he went for it. The event was a smashing success. Even if Nevers was running for State House, to most Zambians he was still their pastor and they had missed seeing him on TV.

In 1996, the media branded Nevers the "dark horse" for the 2001 presidency for they speculated that Zambians might desire a Christian president to follow a Christian president. They were right. Zambian citizens definitely want their third president to be a Christian. The fires of affliction have burned for four trying years. Weaker men would have given up, but not Nevers. He is a man of faith. During this prolonged struggle, Nevers has lost some sleep. During this battle he has also lost some hair. But one thing he has not lost over the past four years is his godly zeal for Zambia. Nevers never gave up because he is a fighter.

10

THE BATTLE IS ON

God spoke clearly into the heart of a young Bemba interpreter that night under the gargantuan yellow tent in Kabwe. After personally witnessing an elderly lady being instantly healed, the Holy Spirit spoke to Nevers' heart, 'my power that healed this lady can change your nation.' That startling epiphany has fueled Dr. Nevers Sekwila Mumba for two decades, as he has endeavored tirelessly to incarnate that 1981 statement. Could it be that the Lord gave Nevers a glimpse that night of what He desired to do through Nevers in Zambia in this new century? Is it possible that God wanted Nevers to see those miracles to let him know that same power would work through him, not only in miracle crusades, but in renovating public policy in a nation that would later be officially dedicated to Christ?

—

Almost twenty years have passed since Nevers and I first met at CFNI. We have lived that entire time on separate continents yet are closer now than ever. It is amazing. Life experience has taught us both the immense value of close friends, so we cherish our friendship as if it was a precious emerald.

As the election nears, I hope Zambians give Nevers a chance to lead their country. It ultimately does not matter whether he runs on the NCC or any other ticket for the party is subsumed by the personality.

In my opinion, Nevers is *the* bridge-builder for a better tomorrow in Zambia:

> *NCC is a party for revolutionaries who believe that if we rise together against injustices and poverty, we can turn the future of our*

nation for the better. I call on all Zambian youth, this is your party for the future. This is the party that shall fight for your welfare, dignity and personal pride.

- *NCC is the bridge from poverty to prosperity.*
- *NCC is the bridge from ignorance to enlightenment.*
- *NCC is the bridge from fear to faith.*
- *NCC is the bridge from one century to another.*

I dream of a Zambia where a car, a home and abundance of food will not be a luxury, but a necessity. I see restoration of dignity and national pride. I see Zambia competing confidently on the international platform of commerce, science, politics and sport. I see a new, healed Zambia in the next century. Some people have asked, "Will Pastor Mumba fight this battle to the end?" If not us, show me who. If not now, show me when. We have put our hands to the plow and we shall not look back. It is too late now. No one can stop us. The battle is on.

For further information, please contact Dr. Mumba directly at:
Box 22656
Kitwe, Zambia
011-260-2-226169 (phone)
or
011-260-96-784585
011-260-2-228032 (fax)
victorym@zamnet.zm
(Zambia is GMT +2)